CREATIVE
WRITING
IN GROUPWORK

There are a thousand thoughts lying within a man that he does not know till he takes up the pen to write.
William Makepeace Thackeray, HENRY ESMOND

CREATIVE
WRITING
IN GROUPWORK

Robin Dynes

WINSLOW

Telford Road • Bicester
Oxon OX6 0TS • UK
Telephone: 01869 244644
Facsimile: 01869 320040

Dedication

This book is dedicated with love to my wife, Jean, who not only understands but has criticised, helped and encouraged. And without whose love and friendship this book would not have been written.

First published in 1988 by
Winslow Press Ltd, Telford Road, Bicester, Oxon OX6 0TS, United Kingdom
www.winslow-press.co.uk
Reprinted 1990, 1991, 1993, 1994, 1996, 1997, 1999

Phototypeset by Gecko Limited, Bicester, Oxon

002-0349/Printed in Great Britain/1010

ISBN 0 86388 066 5

Contents

ROBIN DYNES is currently working in an occupational therapy department of a psychiatric day hospital. His work involves running a variety of groups which include social and creative activities.

Robin has been interested in creative writing all his life. He is a freelance writer, with many non-fiction articles and short stories published in national magazines. He has also been involved in organising, lecturing and running courses in writing at writers' weekend workshops and day schools under the auspices of the local education authority.

Foreword

This book presents a large number of well-tried exercises for creative writing, allowing group members to explore emotions and feelings and enabling them to express themselves.Participants may have had trouble expressing these ideas in the more conventional therapy groups.

What I like so much about the book is the use of so many subjects and variations, which in turn provide the stimulus to create even more ideas on which one can work. Many of the ideas can be developed and adapted, to be used in conjunction with social skills, positive interaction, communication, support and art therapy groups — thereby giving therapists a clearer knowledge and understanding of their clients.

Using these exercises, the author has succeeded in firing the members of his creative writing groups with his own enthusiasm. This is a good comprehensive book which merits shelf space in all occupational therapy departments.

Elizabeth Court, Dip COT SROT
Head Occupational Therapist
Herbert Day Hospital
Bournemouth
Dorset

Acknowledgements

There are few original ideas about writing. The exercises used in this book have been adapted from discussions, ideas and insights shared with writing colleagues over the years and with participants in the various writing groups and classes in which I have taken an active role.

In particular, I am indebted to my wife, Jean, whose long experience and success as a teacher of creative writing in Adult Education has served as inspiration and example. I am grateful for her advice and constant attention while preparing this book.

I would also like to thank the occupational therapists, nurses, doctors, psychologists, social workers, students and helpers with whom I have worked at St Ann's Hospital, Poole, and at Herbert Day Hospital, Bournemouth. All have generously shared their knowledge of groupwork.

Finally, a big thank you to all who have taken part in the groups. I hope their rewards have been as great as mine.

Robin Dynes, 1988

Introduction

Creative writing enables us to find out about ourselves, how we see the world and how the world sees us. It is a journey of self-discovery which helps us to find out what we know, enables us to detach ourselves from experience to examine it, explore situations from other viewpoints, form opinions, solve problems, share insights, compare ideas and develop imagination and creative ability. It is not possible to understand how you feel until you are able to express it in words. This book has been written to help group members find a route to this expression and knowledge.

In *section 1* I have used my own experience to provide suggestions and guidelines for running a writing group. *Section 6* gives advice on producing a magazine or newspaper, the aim being to enable group leaders to use creative writing in an effective way.

Sections 2—5 contain exercises to be used as the basis for group activities. They are designed to probe into our unique way of understanding ourselves and our world and to make accessible thoughts and feelings which can open up a whole new range of possibilities. Careful thought should be given in selecting and adapting the themes to suit the purpose and needs of the group. They can be used to enable people to relax socially or as an aid to development in a therapeutic, teaching, probation, or growth setting.

The book is full of stimulating ideas to be used as source material. It should benefit anyone involved in running activities or personal development programmes: occupational therapists, nurses, those working with guides or scouts, in day centres, social clubs, community centres, education centres, residential centres, churches and so on.

A Guide to Creative Writing in Groupwork

PURPOSE

Creative writing can be used for:
- ▶ fun and enjoyment
- ▶ problem solving
- ▶ positive reinforcement
- ▶ stimulating creative imagination
- ▶ confidence building
- ▶ improving conversational skills
- ▶ exploring feelings
- ▶ building self-awareness
- ▶ creating an awareness of others
- ▶ aiding self-expression
- ▶ building trust
- ▶ breaking social isolation
- ▶ encouraging team-work
- ▶ relieving anxiety
- ▶ developing ideas
- ▶ increasing self-esteem
- ▶ decision making
- ▶ increasing emotional expression
- ▶ improving concentration
- ▶ promoting an ability to explore situations
- ▶ learning to accept ideas from others
- ▶ improving judgement
- ▶ relaxation
- ▶ developing thinking ability
- ▶ exercising memory
- ▶ reality orientation
- ▶ aiding perception and observation
- ▶ social development
- ▶ encouraging awareness of surroundings

BREAKING DOWN BARRIERS TO WRITING

There are many 'built-in' obstacles which can present difficulties to the group leader. These may have originated with preconceived ideas about writing coming from school, parents and past experience. Panic and fear may have to be overcome. Frequent causes of such obstacles are:

a) A belief that grammar, spelling and presentation are of paramount importance;

b) A belief that it is some sort of test which will be analysed and criticised;

c) A belief that everything must be written in a formal manner;

d) A belief that excessive demands are going to be made on creativity and imagination;

e) Unfamiliar surroundings with unfamiliar people combined with ignorance of what is expected.

These fears can be overcome by:

1 Providing a relaxed and appropriate setting. Have enough tables for people to be able to write in comfort without the next person reading over their shoulders. The room should resemble a writing room: books and magazines in view, library leaflets lying about, posters and writing contributions on the walls, typewriters, pens and paper in abundance and so on.

2 Asking the participants what they think will be demanded of them and what they hope to gain. Making it clear that points (a) to (d) are not expected. Discussing the aims and purposes of the group. This not only dispels apprehension but allows members to get to know each other.

3 Choosing for the initial exercises subjects with which the participants will feel comfortable and can succeed.

4 Reading out an example of writing in the same vein, to help clarify what is expected.

5 Discussion before beginning to write. This stimulates the imagination, helps to overcome stock responses and shape what is to be written. However, do not allow more than a few minutes' discussion or the participants will feel that the subject has been 'talked out'. The need to generate and articulate ideas will have been satisfied and writing them down will no longer seem important.

6 Giving the group the widest possible choice in approach and mode of expression. They may write a list of sentences, each one

representing a thought on the subject; use verse, narrative, dialogue or letter format.

7 Not demanding that they write for long periods in complete silence. Whilst unwelcome interruptions are to be discouraged, long periods of absolute silence can create just as much discomfort, especially when participants have short concentration spans. Fifteen minutes of actual writing is adequate for most purposes. The time limit should, of course, be varied to suit the group.

8 Dismissing negative attitudes and thinking by:

▶ Making it understood that derogatory comments or criticisms are not wanted, but alternative points of view or shared experiences are.

▶ Being prepared. Have the room and all materials ready so that writing can begin without interruptions. Make sure that the exercise has been adapted in a way which will create interest, fill needs and not be beyond the capabilities of group members. It should allow them to discover something new about themselves.

▶ Giving an impression of enthusiastic confidence which will discourage negative reactions.

▶ Giving clear instructions about the exercise, the reason for it and what it is intended to do for the participant.

▶ Giving an opportunity for group members to ask questions before writing begins.

9 The leader writing with the group. This breaks down barriers, gives people something to compare and makes the leader more aware of the difficulties.

SELECTING THE EXERCISES

Give thought to the degrees of difficulty of exercises:

Easiest	More Difficult	Hardest
The exercises in which the writers use their own viewpoint and experience.	Writing from other people's viewpoints.	Creating thoughts and dialogue for characters other than themselves.
When the leader presents the group with a given beginning.	When the leader presents the group with an ending, result or solution.	When the leader presents the group with a beginning and an ending and the writer fills in the middle piece.

Bearing the above in mind, the easiest exercises to start with are those dealing with personal experience written from a given beginning. The reasons being:

a) They are experiences the writer knows about, feels comfortable with and can write of with authority;

b) Interest is aroused because these happenings are of maximum importance to the participants;

c) There are definite emotional feelings connected with the events.

For ease of selection, the exercises have been grouped in the following sections:

Section 2 — *General Themes*

Section 3 — *Inspiring the Imagination*

Section 4 — *Exploring Relationships*

Section 5 — *Developing Awareness*

Note that the first five exercises in each section should prove to be the easiest. Also, a large number of the activities, with imagination, can be adapted to fit into more than one section. Whilst all of the exercises can be used in isolation, they are most effective when used as part of a planned strategy, linked from session to session, and in support of other therapeutic or development activities.

CAUTION

When working with disturbed or maladjusted groups bear in mind that:

a) people with identity problems may find writing from other viewpoints distressing;

b) some participants may have difficulty interpreting abstract ideas; and

c) exercises which could act as a stimulant for delusions, etc, should be avoided.

THE DISCUSSION AFTER READING

It is important that everyone gets the opportunity to read out and to comment on other group members' writings if they so wish. Sharing in this way establishes links between different people's perception of experience and promotes confidence. It is also a learning process.

How the group responds will depend on how well they have been prepared and instructed and how clear is the aim and purpose of the exercise to them. Sometimes it is necessary to encourage by example, with the leader making comments to start the discussion. Some guidelines are given with the exercises. However, on most occasions, the discussion should originate from the writing that has been read out. It will find its own direction, dictated by the needs and experiences of group members. Ideally, the response should be:

a) listening with interest;

b) asking questions;

c) sharing group feelings.

The discussion should also be used as feedback, to aid the leader to plan the next session.

CAUTION

Group leaders should not read meanings into or try to carry out an analysis of what has been written. If they do so, they will merely interpret from their own experience — which may have no relation to actuality. They should accept the writing for what it is: a means of expressing views and experiences of the world.

ASSESSMENT OF PROGRESS

The type of assessment will depend on the setting in which the activity takes place. However, there are three main sources which can be used:

1 The leader's observation;

2 The completed work;

3 The participants' assessment of themselves.

In order to assess the members' progress with any accuracy it is necessary initially to establish their expectations and personal goals within the group. This may best be done by getting them to write them down or by giving them a simple questionnaire.

A WIDER AUDIENCE

Sometimes people write solely for their own pleasure but, more often, they wish their writing to have some kind of effect on another person or persons. Usually, both purposes are served. What the writers need to know is thay they have communicated successfully. In order for this to happen they need an audience.

When a sympathetic response is necessary, writing, reading and

7

discussion within the group, as described above, provide a satisfactory forum. However, there is no doubt that providing an even wider readership for appropriate non-personal writing further encourages people to write. If this wider audience is supplied, it means that participants' views and opinions are being noticed, and that gives an enormous boost to confidence and enthusiasm. Here are a few ways of providing this audience:

a) *Reading aloud to an assembled audience.*

b) *Making up folders.* Members can then display their work and loan it out.

c) *Making wall displays, posters, and so on.* Posters with typed poems, cartoons, picture-strips, etc, are good confidence builders. They can be displayed on the walls of the room used by the group to encourage a writing environment.

d) *Producing pamphlets.* Many different types of pamphlets can be introduced. Here are a few examples:
   - ▶ opinions on a subject
   - ▶ poetry
   - ▶ amusing anecdotes
   - ▶ cartoons
   - ▶ comic strips
   - ▶ cookery hints
   - ▶ history of the building or area
   - ▶ local interests, views, walks
   - ▶ gardening hints
   - ▶ hobbies
   - ▶ DIY projects
   - ▶ safety in the home

   If none of the above appeal, ask the group to come up with some subjects, perhaps from their own experience. The pamphlets can be pinned up on the writing room wall and may be sold. Do not forget that many of the exercises in this book, if worked on and shaped, will make pamphlet material.

e) *Producing booklets.* Booklets require a longer time span, a greater sustained effort and more funds. The resulting product is, nevertheless, more rewarding. And booklets can be kept short — for the first effort — or made longer, as desired. Again, writing exercises in this book can be developed and shaped for such use. A mixture of short stories, poems, articles, anecdotes, cartoons and the rest can be utilised to give variety and to ensure that different talents are used within the group.

f) *Producing a magazine or newspaper.* A magazine or newspaper, published on a regular basis, is the biggest commitment both for the group leader and the members. It will mean meeting deadlines for production and collecting enough material each month or quarter, so that readers are not disappointed. Although very demanding and the most difficult to sustain over a long period, this project is probably the most rewarding. It is also the most likely to flag, and therefore fail, if the effort and interest are not maintained after the initial launch.

General Themes

FREEFLOW

PROCEDURE

Ask each person to glance around the room and look out of the window, allowing the mind to take in objects, until something sparks off an association with a familiar event, person or place. The participants write whatever comes into their heads. If that ignites other memories they write those down as well, continuing in this manner for the allowed time.

DISCUSSION

How do people become stimulated to write about something? Is inspiration necessary, or does it come anyway, if you sit down and concentrate? Has writing in this freeflow manner revealed anything present in people's minds of which they were unaware?

ALTERNATIVES

1 Follow up the above exercise by having members pick out one sentence, idea or incident written about, and expand upon it.
2 Have members browse through magazines containing lots of pictures and then write about anything that comes to mind associated with what they have seen.
3 Give starting words, for example: I began . . . I lived . . . Until then . . . I'd forgotten . . . In those days . . . It started . . . Things were different . . . I was only . . . People choose a beginning and write whatever comes into their heads.
4 For ten minutes, write about anything that comes into the mind. Things heard, seen, touched, smelled, tasted; whatever flashes into the mind, no matter how silly or far-fetched.

COMMENT

In writing, getting started is often a barrier. These exercises provide good starting-points and can be practised by participants daily in their own time, which allows them to get used to the idea of sitting writing.

EXPERIENCES

PROCEDURE

Members of the group think about a good experience they have had in the past. This may be a holiday, meeting an old friend, having a meal out, an enjoyable walk and so on. Ask them to recapture the memory by writing about it, including how it made them feel and why it was good.

DISCUSSION

Read out and give everyone an opportunity to say something about each piece. Talk about the importance of sharing experiences and remembering good times.

ALTERNATIVES

Each person writes about:
1   An experience which they would like to have;
2   A bad experience;
3   A surprise;
4   A frightening experience;
5   A happy time in the past;
6   Anticipating an event which does not happen;
7   Being in love;
8   Being lonely.

COMMENT

The variety of experiences is unlimited. If a positive reaction is essential, care should be taken to select the type of subject suitable to the group.

CONTRASTS

PROCEDURE

Examine the difference between two friends. These may be two friends from the present, the past, or someone known years ago compared with a friend from the present. Suggest that the following guidelines are borne in mind:

a) Physical description. What does this show about each friend's character and attitudes?

b) Reasons for the differences in character. Events in their lives which could have influenced them.

c) The type of life the people have led. Are they rich, poor, artistic, career-minded, family oriented, sports-minded?

d) What is it about them that appeals as a friend?

DISCUSSION

Have the group comment on how they feel about what each author has written. Examine some of the things which influence our lives and make us what we are. What is important in friendships? What appeals to each person in a friend?

ALTERNATIVES

Members write contrasting:

1 Two ages: compare being fifteen with being thirty, twenty with being sixty and so on;

2 Two places: this could include, among other possibilities, two houses, two towns, two countries, two beauty spots, area where born with present location of residence;

3 Two ways of doing the same thing;

4 Being popular with being unpopular;

5 Two sisters, brothers, families;

6 Being fit and being unfit;

7 Being a man and being a woman;

8 Being a son and being a father;

9 Being a dog and being a cat;

10 Day and night;

11 The present year and their whole life;

12   The left and right sides of their body, front to back, or top to bottom;

13   Inner and outer experience;

14   Thinking and feeling;

15   Being masculine and being feminine.

COMMENT

The above list gives some idea of the variations which can be used. The possibilities are endless.

CONFLICTS

PROCEDURE

Each participant writes about a conflict they have had with another person. Have them describe what the relationship was before the conflict, how it began, what happened and how it ended.

DISCUSSION

After each author has read out their piece, have other group members comment on how they might have handled the situation. How can conflicts be avoided? Should they always be avoided? Can anyone see how each conflict could have been brought to a more satisfactory conclusion?

ALTERNATIVES

Each person writes about:

1 An inner conflict: a repressed urge, temptation, personal code, loyalty, guilt;
2 A conflict with nature: the sea, the desert, ageing, disease, the weather, time;
3 A conflict with the social aspects of living: politics, religion, beliefs, morality, obligation, legal enforcements, financial situations, customs;
4 A personal conflict with objects: machines, buildings, tools, traffic, furniture;
5 A conflict with other living things: fish, insects, plants, animals, birds, reptiles;
6 A conflict with the supernatural: fate, superstition, God, the devil, good, evil, magic, myth, taboos, antiquity.

COMMENT

Life is full of conflicts. Learning to cope with them is essential to survival. If participants do not want to use their personal conflicts, have them invent some.

ANECDOTES

PROCEDURE

Start the group off by reading out some anecdotes from magazines such as *Readers' Digest*. Each person then writes about an amusing or interesting incident which has happened to them. Encourage the use of artistic licence to exaggerate and enlarge the incident.

DISCUSSION

How does each person's sense of humour differ? Why are some things funny to one person and not another? Pain and misfortune often feature in jokes and humour — why is this?

ALTERNATIVES

1 Write about a misfortune which, in retrospect, seems funny.
2 Base a humorous incident on a clever person or braggart who outsmarts himself and comes to misfortune.
3 Write about moments of acute embarrassment which, in retrospect, are funny.
4 Describe someone who is a funny or amusing character.
5 Tell the story of a goof personally committed or one heard of.

COMMENT

Encourage participants whose anecdotes are really funny to work on them and send them to magazines.

WHAT DO YOU SEE?

PROCEDURE

Cut out a picture from a magazine or other source which depicts people doing something. Examples are: an accident, a crowd on a beach, people at a football match, a courtroom scene or men at work.

Allow the group to study the picture for a few minutes. Then, leaving the picture in sight, ask the participants to write down what they see. Request that they describe everything that is happening in the picture as if they were talking to a friend who has not seen it. Ask them to try to make the scene seem real, as if it is actually happening, and to include the emotions that the people in the picture feel. Remind them to use all the senses: sight, sound, smell, touch and taste. Colour also is often forgotten.

DISCUSSION

Have everyone read out their pieces and compare what has been seen. What has been missed completely? What has been missed by some and seen by others? How has this affected each individual's perception of the picture?

ALTERNATIVES

1 Split the group into pairs. Give each couple a picture. Have them write and then compare what they have seen.
2 Use pictures of objects, animals or scenic views.
3 Take the group outdoors to observe people at play, a shopping centre, people at work on a building site or a scenic view, and have them describe what they observe.

COMMENT

This is an excellent observation exercise and allows participants to compare what they see with what others see. It also generates good interaction.

IMPORTANT PLACES

PROCEDURE

Ask everyone to think of the story of their life as a novel and to recall all the places which have been important in that story. These could include where they were born, grew up, went on a first date, got married, their first home, where they lived.

Each person now describes these places and how they have been influenced by them. Are they remembered as happy, sad, mysterious, alien, cold or warm places? Did the surroundings affect their moods and how they lived? What did each place mean to them? What did they like and dislike about each location? How did each place affect what they did or what happened to them in life?

DISCUSSION

When people have their stories read out, allow the group to consider how places can affect mood, how they live and what they do in life.

ALTERNATIVES

Participants write about:
1   People who have been important in their lives.
2   Jobs which have been important.
3   Holidays in their lives.
4   Unforeseen happenings and surprises they have had in their lives. This could include accidents, gifts, winning the pools, being left property, chance meetings, being made redundant, an opportunity out of the blue, discovering something you own is worth a lot of money and so on.
5   Animals in their lives.
6   Hobbies pursued over the years.

COMMENT

This exercise can turn up some surprises. People often seem to accept a place without being consciously aware of how much effect it has on them.

ALL ABOUT . . .

PROCEDURE

For this exercise, participants write 'all about' a pet subject. Possible subjects are:

backache	being a bore
cruelty to animals	snobbery
family life today	women
making a cake	living in the forties/fifties
ghosts	shopping
adolescence	nagging

DISCUSSION

After each reading, encourage members to share other viewpoints and experiences.

ALTERNATIVES

Each participant writes 'all about':

1 How they have avoided doing a specific job;
2 Something which gives them pleasure and enjoyment;
3 Their worst and best characteristics.

COMMENT

Many other subjects can be added. The exercise provides plenty of scope to write from personal experience; also the topics serve as good subjects for debate.

EMOTIONS & MOODS

PROCEDURE

Ask each member of the group to write about the mood or emotion that is at present dominating their lives. This may be, for example, apathy, anger, hate, love, excitement, impatience, joy. Encourage members to express the emotion. Does it affect their relationships? How they see and interpret the world around them? Does it dominate and disguise their true feelings, allow unimportant things to grow out of proportion? Is it how they want to feel? How do they want to feel? Does it make others misunderstand them?

DISCUSSION

How does mood affect daily living? How does each member of the group cope with moods and emotions in others and in themselves?

ALTERNATIVES

1   Write about changing from one mood to another. Examples:
    sadness to happiness   feeling frightened to feeling secure
    excitement to indifference   feeling listless to feeling ebullient
    hate to love   feeling trapped to feeling free
    anger to calm   feeling lonely to feeling popular
2   Call out a different emotion every five minutes. Each member writes about how if affects them until another emotion is called out. Alternatively, allow each participant to call out an emotion.
3   Write about pleasant or unpleasant memories associated with moods and emotions.
4   Write about recurring emotions and moods.
5   Write about a pleasant and an unpleasant emotion or mood and compare.
6   Write about opposite emotions and moods, such as patience and impatience, apathy and enjoyment, calm and restlessness.

COMMENT

The above examples are given only as a guide. Allow the group freedom to explore their own emotions and feelings.

INTERVIEWS

PROCEDURE

Participants interview one another about their lives, obtaining as much history and background as possible. Include place of birth, family history, children, houses and places lived in, likes and dislikes, ambitions and so on. Once each interview is concluded it is written up to show the person in the best possible light.

DISCUSSION

How did it feel to be interviewed? How difficult was it to be the interviewer? Which came easier? In their write-up, did the interviewers give an accurate picture of the life represented? What information was missing to make it do so?

ALTERNATIVES

1   Each participant interviews one or more of the others to get an opinion on one particular subject. The interviews are then written up.
2   Each person interviews another group member about one particular thing achieved successfully and writes it up.
3   This time, have the participant conduct an interview concerning something the other member would like to do in the future. How do they hope to achieve it?
4   Use an interest, hobby or skill as the subject of the interview.

COMMENT

Make sure that participants interviewed have the opportunity to correct any discrepancies after each reading. The interviews can be conducted on tape and then transcribed. However, if this is done, limit the recording time to a few minutes, otherwise it will run to many pages.

EVERY PICTURE TELLS A STORY

PROCEDURE

Cut out a variety of pictures from magazines. The pictures may be scenic, romantic, contain animals, people doing things, represent notable events, objects, cartoons and so on. Having a wide variety is important. Place these on a table and ask members of the group to select one which seems relevant or appeals to them. It may strike a memory chord, remind them of an unfulfilled dream or prompt thoughts of something they would like to do in the future.

Ask each person to think for a few moments about the picture, allowing their imagination to have full rein, then to begin writing about the memory or wish — telling it as a story that has or might happen.

DISCUSSION

When participants read out their pieces, give ample opportunity for them to expand on what has been written by asking questions. Encourage other members of the group to help by doing likewise and commenting.

ALTERNATIVES

1 Substitute headlines cut from newspapers for the pictures.
2 Use objects. These may be ornaments, toys, pieces of jewellery, household items and so on.
3 Keep the exercise completely imaginative and have everyone make up a story about the picture or object.

COMMENT

Depending on the group, it may be prudent to stipulate that the memory, wish for the future, or story must be something pleasant, positive or humorous — in order to ensure that the exercise is a positive one. Also, to help those who find it difficult, suggest that they pretend they are telling the story to their best friend and write it down accordingly, using the same informal type of language.

SOLVE A PROBLEM

PROCEDURE

Present an appropriate problem or situation to the group. This might be domestic. A mother, along with two small children and a dog, is busy in the kitchen, cooking the evening meal. Suddenly, she realises that one child and the dog are missing and the front door is open. There is a busy road outside. What does she do?

Ask the group to describe the setting and what is happening; how the woman feels, what goes through her mind and what she does to solve the problem; then, having solved it, how she feels about having been careless and the relief experienced afterwards.

DISCUSSION

How has each person differed in the way they saw and handled the situation? What actions were given priority and why? Did this affect the way the situation was handled? Did the woman feel anger? If so, who was it directed at — the dog, the child for running out or herself for leaving the door open? How did this affect the way she handled the situation?

ALTERNATIVES

1 For fun, make the situation comic, ridiculous or a mystery for which a solution has to be provided.
2 Make the situation a serious one, but with a comic or absurd outcome, or vice versa.
3 Use for problem solving. Think up the type of situations or problems with which the group need to be able to cope.
4 Ask each person to describe a problem they have had or a situation they have found themselves in and how they resolved it.
5 Cut out situations from the problem pages of women's magazines and ask the group to imagine themselves in each situation and to describe what they would do to resolve it.

COMMENT

If anyone has difficulty describing how the woman feels, it sometimes helps to have the exercise written in the first person. The writers would then imagine that they are the woman and that everything is happening to them.

FIRST EXPERIENCES

PROCEDURE

For this exercise, request that each person relaxes and thinks about when they had an experience for the first time. This may be their first day at school, first day in hospital, first time on holiday, first time they fell in love, a first date, a first friend, the first suit or dress they had, their first car, the first time they went swimming and so on.

Suggest that they recapture the way they felt, what impressions they had, what the experience meant to them and how important it was. Ask them to write it all down as if it is happening now, at this moment.

DISCUSSION

Is there any difference between a first experience and any other? What makes this so? Which members enjoy first experiences and which find themselves subject to anxiety on these occasions? How does this affect their impression of the experience, how they remember it, how they handle the situation and their willingness to do new things?

ALTERNATIVES

1   Use last day experiences, such as a last day in hospital, last day at school, last day in a job, last day in a house, the last time they did something.

2   Request that each person writes about an experience that made a lasting impression, or one that they remember with pride. Winning a prize, raising money for charity, helping a friend, are examples.

COMMENT

It can help to aid the memory of these occasions if everyone is reminded to use the five senses. What sights, sounds, smells, sensations of touch and taste can they recall?

THE FIVE SENSES

PROCEDURE

Take the group for a short walk. Instruct them to concentrate on the sense of sight. Make sure that there is plenty to see on the journey. Tell the participants that you want them to observe everything that is happening. When the walk is completed, ask everyone to write, describing what they have seen using colour, shade, light, movement and so on. The narrative should conjure up pictures like a silent movie.

DISCUSSION

Compare individual observations and what has been missed. Talk about seeing and appreciating what is around us and why some people appear to see more than others.

ALTERNATIVES

1 This time, instruct members to use the sensation of touch as they walk. Have them touch and examine objects, vegetation, animals and so on.

2 Hand out various things to eat or taste on the walk. How does the sense of taste change on the journey?

3 Concentrate on the sense of hearing during the walk. Alternatively, use a recording of various sounds.

4 Lastly, use smell. What is repellent? What is pleasant? What can be learned from the various smells and what sensations do they give?

COMMENT

This set of exercises is best done as a series which helps participants to appreciate and use all the senses in order to communicate feeling and experience. Alas, today we live in a one- or two-dimensional world, using mostly sight. These exercises help to expand that world.

PUZZLER

PROCEDURE

Participants search their past to remember a person whom they misjudged or misunderstood. Later, because of something found out, an explanation or some action on the part of that person, they came to realise the error of the initial judgement. For example, the person may have been thought to be generous but was mean, cruel but found to be kind, helpful but was really misleading for his own benefit.

Ask members to:

a) Describe the person briefly. Indicate what they thought and felt about them, giving details of what they did, said and so on that was misleading. Do not, at this stage, reveal the misunderstanding.

b) Describe what happened to make them change their minds about this person and explain the error of judgement.

c) Lastly, describe what effect the realisation had on them. How did they feel? How did it change their opinion about — and relationship with — the person? Did it spur them into any actions or lead them to form any philosophy about the incident?

DISCUSSION

Why was the mistake made? Were there any clues that might have been noticed or taken into account to avoid the error? What ideas did they have that were wrong? Could the error have been avoided? Did it tell them anything about themselves?

ALTERNATIVES

1 Participants describe a situation in which they were misunderstood;

2 Use an accident or happening where the truth is not as it might appear — a misunderstood situation;

3 Participants think of a problem they had but could not solve because of misunderstanding it.

COMMENT

This exercise can be a source of really good fun.

A SENSE OF PLACE

PROCEDURE

On a blackboard or large sheet of paper, print a number of familiar place names, such as garden, park, playground, kitchen, bedroom, lounge, hall, bathroom, dining-room. Ask group members to choose one or two words from the list and write about the events or things which, in their minds, are associated with each place. Encourage them to draw on childhood memories.

DISCUSSION

Do people feel more comfortable in certain rooms and areas than in other places? Compare the type of behaviour and family conflicts which group members associate with certain areas. Do the associations influence present-day thoughts about them?

ALTERNATIVES

1 Call out the words in the list one at a time and have group members write for five minutes on each;

2 Ask participants to write about the room or place they would like to have — and the behaviour and effect they would want it to generate.

COMMENT

It is surprising how much detail and memory these words can evoke. Memories, when recalled, can help to clarify present attitudes.

JOURNEYS

PROCEDURE

Ask group members to write about a journey they have made recently. This may be a simple trip to the shops or a long journey from one end of the country to the other. Instruct them to write about it as if they have just arrived and are telling a friend about the difficulties encountered, people met and things seen and heard on the journey.

DISCUSSION

Compare different people's attitudes to travel and how this affects the journey. What else can influence whether or not the journey is an enjoyable one? How do people cope with problems encountered while travelling?

ALTERNATIVES

Members write about:
1   A memorable or favourite journey.
2   An imagined journey that they would like to make.
3   A journey they would not like to make, giving the reason.
4   The start of a journey, up to the point when a difficulty is encountered. The story is then passed on to the person on the left who continues the story until the next problem arises. The story is then passed on again. This continues until everyone has added a bit to each journey.

COMMENT

Experiment by having people write in different moods. One person writes excitedly about a journey, another in a state of anxiety, another bored by it, another having been forced to make the journey, yet another in a state of exhaustion, and so on. Afterwards, compare how the moods have affected the journey.

CHANGES

PROCEDURE

Members write about a person they have met, a friend or an associate who has changed, destroyed or enlarged their understanding or concept of something. Have them state the original viewpoint held, how the person influenced it and what it changed into. Include some description of the person and the impact this change has had on the writer's life.

DISCUSSION

How do others influence our lives? When is such influence good and when is it bad? Talk about how to resist being bullied into accepting viewpoints or things you do not want to do. How does seeing things from another angle change us and our vision of the world? Is change inevitable?

ALTERNATIVES

Each participant writes about:

1   A new place visited which, when they arrived, was different from what they had expected. This could be a holiday place, a hospital, a place of work and so on.
2   Something that happened which changed how they saw things. Perhaps an accident, some good luck, discovering something, an act of kindness, or something similar.

COMMENT

Life and ideas around us are constantly changing. This exercise promotes discussion about ways of coping with these changes.

MEETING THE UNKNOWN

PROCEDURE

In this exercise, group members write about meeting a person who is unknown to them. This may be a stranger on a train, someone who is going to interview them, a neighbour's relative, a doctor, a nurse, a new postman and so on. Ask each person to describe how they felt before the meeting, the reaction during the meeting and afterwards. Encourage the use of dialogue, some description of the place and the new acquaintance.

DISCUSSION

Compare each person's experience. How did attitudes, place and reason for the meeting affect the outcome? If the meeting was not a satisfactory one, can members of the group see how and why this happened and suggest other ways of handling the situation?

ALTERNATIVES

Participants write about:

1   Going to an unknown place, such as a hospital, police station, airport, or another country.
2   Facing a new problem, a new idea or making a decision without the facts being fully understood or when the outcome cannot be foreseen. Examples might include events such as taking on a new job with which you are not sure you can cope, or moving home to an unfamiliar area.

COMMENT

These are anxieties everyone faces and has to cope with in daily living. Often there are no answers and the anxieties are healthy reactions. Discussing and sharing the experience can be reassuring and supportive.

SECRETS

PROCEDURE

Invite group members to write about a secret that they have had in the past. It might be something simple, like keeping a surprise party secret, something known about a friend, some error made or lie told. Each person should tell the story of how the secret came about, what it was, how it was kept or not kept — and how keeping a secret felt.

DISCUSSION

Do most people have secrets? What difficulties can secrets present? Should people have secrets, or should they always be open, frank and honest?

ALTERNATIVES

Participants write about:
1   Being kept out of a secret;
2   Famous secrets or scandals in fact or fiction;
3   A secret they would like to have;
4   A secret they would hate to have.

COMMENT

This exercise can turn up some gems and is great fun.

CHOICE

PROCEDURE

Participants imagine they are going to a party. They know someone who is going to pick a fight with them will be there. Give each group member a different course of action which could be taken in the situation. They then write up an account of what happened, the end result, and state what they felt about the outcome. Suggested courses of action:

a) go home;
b) try to reason with the other person;
c) hit the other person first;
d) pretend the other person does not exist;
e) take someone else along to intervene;
f) inform the host or the police;
g) go somewhere else.

DISCUSSION

Discuss the desirability of various outcomes. Is there a choice of action in most situations? Can the same process of selection be applied to problems in life, if time is taken to assess them?

ALTERNATIVES

Apply a similar process of selection to:

1   Returning to a job where the participant has done something wrong or disgraced themself.
2   Facing a husband, wife or friend with whom the person is no longer on speaking terms.
3   Meeting someone who bullies or embarrasses the participant.
4   Facing a group of people to whom the participant feels obliged to give a thank-you speech, but feels too shy or nervous to do it.

COMMENT

Make up other 'Choice' situations to suit the requirements of the participants. Start the group off by having members call out various courses of action for the situation.

PROCEDURE

Group members imagine that they have committed some breach of discipline at work which has resulted in an accident, loss of business or something going wrong. They write an account of what happened as they would tell it to their employer or manager. Then they write a second version, this time as though they were confiding in a good and trusted friend.

DISCUSSION

What changes have been made in the way the account has been told? How has the language altered? What has been added, left out and so on? Do both people hearing the story understand the same thing from it? Can anyone think of an incident in real life when they have slanted something in this way? Discuss the ethics of slanting information.

ALTERNATIVES

1   Write about an incident or accident, first for an adult reader; then rewrite for a child.
2   Imagine you have been involved in an incident of heroism. Write a report of it, to be published in the local newspaper. Now rewrite the same story as you would tell it to your husband or wife, expressing fear and so on.
3   Write an account of an accident as you would tell it to a friend imparting bad news about something concerning them. Rewrite the account as you would present it to someone who caused the accident and whom you dislike.

COMMENT

Daily, when communicating, we edit, censor, leave out and highlight information. The same incident retold is often given many different meanings, frequently leading to misunderstanding and confusion. The above exercise demonstrates how this comes about.

EDITORIAL

PROCEDURE

For this exercise participants envisage themselves as the editor of the first issue of a new magazine being published on their favourite hobby or interest. They write an editorial expressing their views and appreciation of the hobby, what benefits they derive from it and what it can do for the readers.

DISCUSSION

What interest has each editorial created in the other members? Can each editor state the benefits other group members would derive from taking up the interest? Do the others agree? Does the same interest give the same benefits to each person pursuing it, or do different people derive different benefits?

ALTERNATIVES

Participants write an editorial for:

1 A magazine produced by the group;
2 A family magazine;
3 A popular newspaper;
4 A health magazine;
5 A magazine about the royal family;
6 A children's magazine;
7 A magazine for retired people;
8 A political magazine.

COMMENT

It is helpful to read out an editorial from a magazine of the type selected before participants begin to write. The above list is only a small sample of the vast range of magazine types available. If none can be found to suit the needs of the group, invent one of your own.

PROCEDURE

Cut out some controversial articles or items of news from newspapers or magazines. Ask each participant to select one about which they have strong opinions. They read the article, then write in reaction to it, giving vent to their emotions – whether in appreciation or anger. Examples of subjects for news items: blood sports, disarmament, women's rights, cruelty to children, cruelty to animals, destruction of the environment and so on.

DISCUSSION

What was it in each selected news item that made each person react in the way they did? Was it a reasonable and understandable reaction, given the person's viewpoint? Did any reaction show intolerance of the journalist's opinions and an unwillingness to listen to another viewpoint? Did anyone who agreed with the article feel pleased by confirmation of their own opinion? Why? Does any of the above indicate anything about the need to keep in touch with what is happening in the world and the opinions of other people? Why do we feel such a need?

ALTERNATIVES

Participants write in reaction to:
1   A television or radio programme seen or heard recently;
2   A book read;
3   A play or show seen;
4   A new song or musical fad which is popular;
5   Something which is of concern to the participants' own locality;
6   Something which is happening in society and is of concern to members, such as changes in education, unemployment, taxation, the rise in crime and violence, privatisation, lack of morality.

COMMENT

Read out an article to the group, watch a television programme or listen to a radio play and then have participants write an appreciation or criticism. Compare and share opinions.

SYMBOLISM

PROCEDURE

Place some objects on a table. Examples: a clock, a piece of leather, a selection of toys, a whistle, a paperweight, pieces of jewellery, holiday mementos, an old shoe, a piece of velvet and so on. Provide a fairly wide choice. Ask participants to select one object which symbolises something from their lives. They then write about what it symbolises.

DISCUSSION

Encourage participants to ask questions, show interest and help each person who reads out their piece to expand and express this part of their life.

ALTERNATIVES

1 Use geometric drawings instead of objects. Examples: circles, triangles, squares, rectangles, ovals, cubes, octagons, penta-grams. Participants pick out a shape which symbolises something from their lives.

2 Use a selection of colour cards. Group members pick out a colour which symbolises something from their lives.

COMMENT

If it is necessary to keep the thoughts of participants positive ask them to use only pleasant associations.

IMPROMPTU THEMES

PROCEDURE

Give the group a theme to write about, say, for example, success. Make a list of associated words and phrases, such as luxury, fame, piece of luck, attainment, triumph, stroke of genius, coup, easy street. Each person selects from the list or the leader calls out one word every five minutes. Instruct group members to write down whatever comes into their heads spontaneously.

DISCUSSION

Compare experiences of success and how these experiences have influenced behaviour and attitudes.

ALTERNATIVES

Participants write about:

1 Special times of the year such as Easter, Christmas, New Year, Hallowe'en;
2 Birthdays, centenaries and anniversaries;
3 Winter, autumn, spring and summer;
4 Words associated with the cycle of life, like birth, childhood, teens, middle age, old age, death.

COMMENT

Unending lists of words can be made up from a variety of themes. Bear the age and interests of the group members in mind when making up lists less general than the above.

DIARIES

PROCEDURE

Give group members a sheet of paper with the days of the week written down one side and a space between each, as in a diary. Ask each person to make an entry for each day and thereby compile a typical week in their lives. For example:

Monday: Back to work — dead boring! Met John for lunch. He's broke again. Mum's right, he just sponges off me. Played tennis with Jane after work. She says I should change my job if I hate it so much.

Participants continue in the same manner for the remaining days of the week.

DISCUSSION

Do any group members keep a diary? How does it help them? Why have famous people kept diaries? Can we learn anything about ourselves from keeping one of our own? Discuss different reasons for keeping a diary.

ALTERNATIVES

Have each participant write a similar weekly diary from the viewpoint of:

1   a shop assistant;
2   a newspaper reporter;
3   a famous person;
4   a fictional character;
5   themselves, depicting the sort of life they would like to lead.

COMMENT

The diaries can be read out anonymously, giving the group an opportunity to comment on how they imagine the author. Many other alternatives can be added. It is better to begin with occupations with which the participants are familiar, and then progress to an appreciation of other lifestyles.

SHARING KNOWLEDGE

PROCEDURE

Ask each person to think about something of which they have a special knowledge. This may be a job they have done, a skill, a hobby, a subject they know about, or a special — perhaps different — way of doing something. Participants then write about this special knowledge, in order to share it with the group.

DISCUSSION

Ask participants how it feels to be able to share this knowledge with the group. Does it give a good feeling? Discuss the benefits of being able to learn from others and the reasons why we should share our knowledge. How do books, radio and television affect the ability to share knowledge?

ALTERNATIVES

Participants think of and write about:
1 A personal experience of dealing with a friend, which could help other people overcome a similar problem.
2 An experience of dealing with a problem at work, which could help others to cope in similar circumstances.
3 An experience within the family, which could help others faced with the same difficulty.

COMMENT

The alternatives work better when there has been time to build up confidence and trust within the group.

PROCEDURE

Have the group members discuss a subject such as 'ghosts' for a few minutes. This can include personal experiences, belief, disbelief, legends, personal ghosts which haunt participants from the past and so on. After they have been stimulated, ask members to write a short article, story, anecdote or poem, with 'ghosts' as the theme.

DISCUSSION

Who believes in ghosts and who does not? What has led members to believe as they do? Share feelings and experiences of unexplained happenings. Can rational explanations always be found? Is guilt behind any experience of personal ghosts?

ALTERNATIVES

Participants discuss very briefly and then write in the same manner about:

1	Marriage	5	An unusual occupation
2	The sea	6	Naivety
3	Prejudice	7	Kindness
4	Revenge	8	Loneliness

COMMENT

The above reflects the variety of themes which can be written about in this manner — many more can be added.

Inspiring the Imagination

ONE BEAUTIFUL MORNING

PROCEDURE

Group members imagine themselves out in the country. It is a beautiful spring morning and they have had a good night's rest. Birds can be heard, perhaps a deer can be seen bathing in the morning sun. Members describe the morning, what they see, hear, smell and feel as they walk in the country.

DISCUSSION

Read out what has been written and share each person's imagination. Compare ideas of a beautiful morning. What appeals to some and not to others? Explore the reasons.

ALTERNATIVES

1   Imagine being an animal, an object or a plant on such a morning.
2   Have each member imagine being visited by an image of himself on a beautiful morning. He then writes from the viewpoint of the image, giving impressions and thoughts about the visit, the morning and the participant.
3   Change the setting. Make the scene a tropical island, a safari park, the town or city, by a lake, in the mountains and so on.
4   Use the above alternatives in any pleasant situation. This may be, for example, a beautiful evening, a mid-summer day, or the first day of spring.

COMMENT

If anyone says they cannot write in this manner, encourage them to write a list of what they see, hear, smell and feel. This is a delightful exercise which is positive and uplifting. If necessary, point out that only positive or humorous thoughts are to be expressed.

HEROIC DEEDS

PROCEDURE

For this exercise participants imagine themselves as a hero or heroine performing some brave deed. This can be an act needing physical stamina, moral fibre or a great sacrifice. It may also be a true story. People write the story, describing the emotions they experienced before, during and after the brave act.

DISCUSSION

How different do people see themselves as being before and after the incident? Would other people's opinion of them change after an heroic act? Encourage members to talk about any such deeds they may have done or have read about.

ALTERNATIVES

Group members write about themselves as:

1 A criminal or someone who has done something wrong;
2 A person who has given a large donation or organised something for charity;
3 Someone who has received charity;
4 A person who has achieved a lifelong ambition;
5 Someone who has set themselves a task and failed.

COMMENT

Again, there is no limit to the variations which can be thought up on this theme. It is often a good idea to have half the group writing on the positive side and the other half on the negative. Alternatively, do them in successive sessions.

BEGINNING SENTENCES

PROCEDURE

Give a beginning sentence from which everyone must continue in order to write a story, poem, article or whatever they wish. Either write out a selection of sentences, from which one can be chosen by each participant, or give just one sentence as a starting-point. Here are a few suggestions:

I saw the curtain move slightly.

The girl looked frightened.

Peace came, like calm before a storm.

Suddenly, the bird swooped.

He stared at the writing on the envelope.

She heard footsteps behind her.

DISCUSSION

Have the group members comment and suggest ways of improving and developing the piece of writing.

ALTERNATIVES

1   Use a picture or pictures in place of a beginning sentence.
2   Use titles or headlines cut from newspapers or magazines for inspiration.
3   Play music, as food for the imagination.
4   Have participants invent possible origins for everyday phrases.
    Examples:

    getting down to brass tacks   out of the wood
    could have died laughing   driving a hard bargain
    saved by the bell   nine days' wonder
    pretty kettle of fish   a baker's dozen

5   Provide a list of superstitions and have group members select one. They then invent an origin or tale which demonstrates its truth or untruth. Examples:

    Finding a pin is a lucky omen.
    Breaking a mirror brings seven years' bad luck.
    Walking under a ladder is unlucky.
    Touch wood for luck.
    Happy is the bride that the sun shines on.

COMMENT

It is amazing how many different ideas can be inspired by the same sentence, picture and so on.

TALL STORIES

PROCEDURE

Have participants invent a tall story from something which happened to them. They add to the incident, exaggerating it until it becomes fiction. They then write their tall story, stretching credibility to its limits. Encourage people to attempt to create a single effect of horror, comedy, sympathy or whatever it might be in the reader.

DISCUSSION

Have group members state what they think was the single effect the writer was trying to create. Did it work? How could it have been developed further, in order to improve it?

ALTERNATIVES

Participants write tall stories about:

1   Strange dreams;
2   Unsocial behaviour;
3   A protest at an injustice;
4   The sadness of things;
5   An irreverance;
6   A forewarning of a coming event.

COMMENT

This exercise really does bring out a sense of fun and good humour.

FANTASY WISH

PROCEDURE

Each group member thinks of a fantasy wish — the more fantastic the better. They then describe how they would achieve it and how it would feel.

DISCUSSION

What does it feel like to work for something and then achieve it? Which is the most enjoyable:

a) anticipating what success will be like;
b) working for it;
c) having achieved it?

Is there any difference between what we think success will be like and how it really is?

ALTERNATIVES

1 Describe a fantasy romance, adventure or journey.
2 If each participant could have something from a shop that would change their life, what would it be and how would it do so?
3 If each member moved to a new home which had an attic in which they were to discover a precious object, what would it be and why?
4 If members could leave a precious object in an attic for someone to find, what would it be and why?
5 Everyone writes about a fantasy present they would like to give or receive.

COMMENT

Many more alternatives can be added. There is no need to stick to logic or feasibility.

HIGH IN THE SKY

PROCEDURE

Participants imagine themselves up in an aircraft, ready to make a parachute jump. What do they see, feel and hear? As they look down on the fields and houses below, do things appear very much different from the way they are normally seen? As they jump and descend, what sensations are felt? Describe the imaginary experience.

DISCUSSION

Does looking at things from a different angle, as from an aircraft, give a different perspective or understanding? Why? Does this apply to ideas, situations, problems and the like? How can different angles be found for such things as problems or ideas? Has any group member been up in an aircraft or made a parachute drop? Share experiences.

ALTERNATIVES

Participants write, imagining being:
1 Deep down in the earth, in a cave or mine;
2 Underneath the sea, in a submarine;
3 In outer space, in a satellite, looking down on the earth.

COMMENT

These are good ideas for encouraging the use of poetry or verse as a form of expression.

SHAPE OF THINGS TO COME

PROCEDURE

Participants pick something which will, or could, become obsolete in the future, such as rail travel, cars, money as we know it or books. They describe the subject and its function. Then they write about what will replace it and how this will operate. Participants should come up with their own inventions and indicate both the personal and social outcome from them.

DISCUSSION

Do members resist new ideas? Is this because they do not understand them or because they want things to remain the same? Why is this not always possible? Compare attitudes. Discuss the importance of keeping up-to-date with events and being prepared for change.

ALTERNATIVES

Participants write about:

1 Areas reflecting change during their lifetime. These might include decimalisation, sanitation, methods of heating the home, introduction of television, modes of travel and so on. Include the personal and social outcome of the changes.

2 Something in their own life which they fear might change and the dreaded outcome.

3 Political changes — past, present or future — and their personal and social effects.

4 Changes in attitudes — past, present or future — and their personal and social effects.

5 Changes in family life — past, present and anticipated — and their personal and social effects.

COMMENT

These exercises are useful in helping people consider and prepare for change.

STORY IN A BAG

PROCEDURE

Give each person some objects in a bag and ask them to write a story or sketch which features all the objects. Three items in each bag should suffice for most groups but, depending on the abilities of the group, more can be used. For a really imaginative group and a fun approach, choose objects which will be difficult to link logically. To make the exercise low-key, choose items more easily linked together.

DISCUSSION

Encourage each member of the group to comment on the stories as they are read out, bearing in mind the lack of logic, imaginative and fun approach adopted by some — and the more concrete, logical approach of others. Discuss ways in which the latter might limit the imagination and the former might lead to unrealistic attitudes. Ask if members are prepared to accept an illogical or absurd story because it is entertaining and discuss the answers.

ALTERNATIVES

1 Use three items only. Place them in the centre of a table and ask each member to write their own story linking the three objects. Everyone will come up with a different story.
2 Ask participants to write the stories in play form, using dialogue only. These can then be performed, with different members of the group taking the parts.
3 As well as giving three objects to be linked, stipulate a theme, such as a romance, a murder, science fiction or comedy.

COMMENT

A stimulating exercise for the imagination which provides a lot of fun.

MAROONED

PROCEDURE

Group members envisage themselves shipwrecked or crashed in a foreign land, on an island or deep in the jungle. It must be a place where they do not understand the language or culture of the native people, to whom they are also strange. Participants describe how they feel at meeting a strange people, what they think, how they communicate and how they get the natives to co-operate and help them. Suggest that the story is written as an adventure with the hosts' initial reaction being one of anger or fright.

DISCUSSION

Compare how each person has coped. Discuss non-verbal communication and ways of making unsympathetic people understand. Have any group members assumed intellectual superiority? Why? What difficulties can this lead to?

ALTERNATIVES

1   Reverse roles — the group member becomes the host. Someone from an unknown culture arrives in a similar manner on his home ground. What happens?

2   The participants imagine themselves as space travellers, who land on an unknown planet and meet another intelligence.

3   Have the group members imagine that they have to make a long journey with their alien host or visitor. Have them write about the trip. What problems are encountered and how are they overcome?

COMMENT

Do the above as a series of exercises or split the group into sections to do alternatives.

FANTASY JOURNEY

PROCEDURE

Participants pretend they are on a magic carpet. It rises, hovers and takes them safely over mountains and seas to a paradise. It is somewhere they have always wanted to go or an imaginary place. The carpet descends and they explore the area. Who do they meet? What do they see? Have each person describe an hour or a day spent there, ending with climbing back onto the carpet and returning to everyday life.

DISCUSSION

What is there in each paradise that cannot be experienced in real life? Why? Are there any ambitions revealed? How different is each member's idea of paradise? Why is this so? Does anything written reflect what each person wants from real life?

ALTERNATIVES

1 Instead of a carpet, use a time machine which transports each person to a historical period they would like to have lived in.
2 Transport individuals forward in time a few years, or into the next century, and have them write about the sort of life they imagine they might live in that period.
3 Transport each participant to a planet where life is lived as they would like it to be. Have them describe this world, how life would be lived there, comment on values and so on.

COMMENT

Some effort put into creating atmosphere for the journey is helpful in sparking inspiration for this exercise.

PICTURE STORIES

PROCEDURE

Cut out a good selection of picture stories and cartoon strips from magazines or newspapers. Blot out the dialogue bubbles and story line with blank labels or by some other means. Ask each person to select one item and then write up the story as they interpret it.

DISCUSSION

Allow members of the group to react to each story and make alternative suggestions.

ALTERNATIVES

1   Cut out lots of photographs of royalty from magazines and paste them on a large sheet in some sort of sequence. Draw dialogue bubbles on them and have the group make up what is being said and a story-line. To make this exercise easier, do comment bubbles on each picture and use separately without a story-line. Also, use pictures of the Prime Minister, presidents or any famous people in this way.
2   Using old Christmas cards, build up a Christmas story as in (1) above.
3   From a wide selection of pictures cut at random, have each person choose a few which can be loosely linked by a story-line.

COMMENT

This exercise is terrific fun with the whole group contributing to one story-line. Also, have one member of the group fill in one picture of the strip and then pass it on to the next member who continues the story, and so on, round the group. This way a chain of several stories, equal to the number of people in the group, can be passing round at the same time.

PICTURE FRAME STORIES

PROCEDURE

Draw a rectangle six inches by nine inches on a blank sheet of paper and then divide into six squares. Number the squares or frames 1 to 6. Draw a picture in frame 1 showing a situation, and an ending in frame 6. Rough outlines or figures cut from pictures and stuck on will do. Photocopy and hand out to the group. Everyone now thinks of a story to fit his series of frames. Encourage sketching inside the frames to get the imagination going. Matchstick people will suffice for those who will not attempt to draw. Finally, have each person add word bubbles and write in the dialogue to his story-line.

DISCUSSION

Pass each story to all group members. Talk about the various story-lines and the different way each person interpreted and solved the problem.

ALTERNATIVES

1 Give only a beginning, an ending or a theme for the story. Theme examples: jealousy, ambition, love, loyalty and so on.

2 Divide the participants into small groups and have each group work on a story-line.

3 Allow complete imaginative freedom by leaving all the frames blank and giving no theme. Bear in mind that this is very difficult for some people.

COMMENT

The finished pictures can be coloured to give extra satisfaction.

HISTORICAL FARCE

PROCEDURE

Make a list of historical characters from all ages. Group members select two or three characters and make up an incident, story or conversation illustrating what might have happened if these people had met in real life. Characters might include Queen Boadicea, Lord Nelson, Buffalo Bill, Mary Queen of Scots, Queen Victoria, Helen of Troy, Alexander the Great, Cleopatra, Abraham Lincoln or Winston Churchill. Before anyone begins to write, it is a good idea to familiarise the group with the characters by discussing them for a few minutes.

DISCUSSION

Talk about the way each character influenced history for good or bad. What were the qualities that made them outstanding? If any of the characters had met in real life would it have changed the course of history? How and why?

ALTERNATIVES

1   Make two lists: one of historical characters and another of present day politicians, writers, entertainers and so on. Group members select at least one character from each list and write, imagining what the characters would say or do if it was possible for them to meet.

2   Do as in (1) above, but this time make a list of real people and also one of fictional characters from books, television or films.

3   Do any of the above alternatives as a play. Split people into groups of three to five and let each person write the part of one character.

COMMENT

It is a good idea to have a history book handy to sort out any major historical disagreements which become the subject of discussion. For other alternatives see *Conversations*, p65.

CASTAWAY

PROCEDURE

Ask each participant to write about how they became a castaway in an unknown place. This could be a new, undiscovered land mass, an island which has suddenly appeared, or a planet in space. Have them tell about the terrain of the place, how they survived and lived each day, who was with them, what adventures they had and what rules were made. Include details of how they dealt with the situation when these rules were broken and how they were rescued.

DISCUSSION

After each piece has been read out encourage other group members to ask questions about the way various difficulties were overcome. Talk about different ways of dealing with the problems.

ALTERNATIVES

1   Each person writes a poem about the undiscovered island or planet. Allow freedom in this or suggest shape-poetry, written inside silhouette outlines of the island or animals, for example, on the planet.
2   Divide the members into small groups of three or four people. Then have each group write a short play, with individuals writing their own parts in a 'castaway' adventure.
3   Everyone writes a letter to be put in a bottle or sent through space telling of their plight and why they should be rescued.
4   Each participant writes about the unknown place, years after their adventure, when they have bought it and are trying to sell it as a holiday resort.

COMMENT

Display pictures showing islands, unusual scenery, landscapes and science fiction art to help stimulate the imagination.

FAMILIAR PLACES

PROCEDURE

Participants recall a place with which they are familiar. This can be a favourite spot, somewhere they dislike, their home, a beach, a country walk and so on. Ask them to write a story or recount an incident, using the atmosphere and emotive feeling of the familiar place as inspiration. Encourage the use of description to colour the mood of the story.

DISCUSSION

Could the sense of atmosphere be enriched by more use of the five senses? Has colour been used in the description? What is suggested to the other group members by the atmosphere described? Have members share their experiences of familiar places. Does the familiarity detract from or add to the appreciation of them? Does the familiarity help to give a sense of security or dislike?

ALTERNATIVES

Participants write a story or describe an incident in which:
1　A person they know plays an important part;
2　An animal, with which they are familiar, features;
3　Wind and rain or a storm is the cause of what happens;
4　A well known superstition influences what happens.

COMMENT

It helps to read out a short piece of description which demonstrates the use of atmosphere and background. The beginning of *The Fall of the House of Usher*, by Edgar Allan Poe, is a classic example.

IMPROBABLE SITUATIONS

PROCEDURE

Think up a number of improbable situations, such as being stranded in a snowbound train on a mountain pass with someone famous you detest, or having to serve tea to royalty without knowledge of protocol. If possible, give group members the opportunity to help in compiling these situations. Now give each person a situation and have them write down a reasonable and logical explanation of how they came to be in that predicament and how they handled it.

DISCUSSION

Which story is the most plausible and best explanation of the situation? Can group members think of alternative explanations to the one being read out? Could the situation have been avoided? How?

ALTERNATIVES

1　Have group members write about improbable situations they have experienced.
2　Do some research and list famous improbable situations and scandals or take some from novels. Let group members provide explanations.
3　Ask each person to make up an improbable situation which they would find funny or would like to be in. Now members exchange situations with each other and write up explanations for the predicament they have been given.

COMMENT

Emphasise that explanations must have some sort of logic. Saying that it was done for a bet or a dare is not acceptable.

NONSENSE ESSAY

PROCEDURE

Group members write a nonsense essay, talk, poem or story on a subject or theme selected from a list presented to them. Examples:

a)   The experiences of a flea-training expert.
b)   How to earn a living by painting the sky.
c)   Why people should abandon the earth.
d)   'Living on the Edge', by a flat earth society member.
e)   A gnome preservation appeal by a gnome.

DISCUSSION

How persuasive and inventive are the stories? Can group members help improve each development? How did it feel writing nonsense? Was it fun? Did anyone feel silly, have a fear of looking foolish, stupid or falling flat? Compare feelings about this in the group and ways of coping with it.

ALTERNATIVES

Participants write about:

1   A ridiculous discovery;
2   A stupid or absurd invention;
3   A theory of very doubtful origin;
4   An unbelievable outlook or way of life.

COMMENT

This is an enjoyable way of having people experience being silly, then discovering that life goes on afterwards.

TRAITS

PROCEDURE

From newspapers and magazines cut out photographs of individuals. Invite each group member to choose one and ask them to give a trait to the character in the selected picture. They then explain in writing how the person came to have the trait and how it has influenced the character's life. Examples of traits are:

gullibility	meanness	inquisitiveness
untidiness	over-confidence	telling lies
bad manners	stinginess	clumsiness
timidity	keenness	selfishness
liveliness	perfectionist	greediness

DISCUSSION

Discuss the predicaments and problems various traits could lead one into. When are the traits an advantage and when a disadvantage? How are such traits formed in people? Can something be done about a harmful trait?

ALTERNATIVES

1 Have each group member write about a personal trait and the effect it has had on their life.
2 Participants write about a dominant trait in a friend and the effect it has had on their relationship, good or bad.
3 Members choose a well known personality and write about a trait which they think has influenced his success.

COMMENT

If desired, writing can be restricted to positive traits.

THE CONSPIRATORS

PROCEDURE

Present the group with the above title. Ask them what it conjures up in their minds? What type of people, what type of activities? Can they imagine a conspiracy taking place? Group members now imagine themselves to be involved in a conspiracy, describing how they became involved, why, what happened and what was the outcome.

DISCUSSION

Which members have shown themselves as innocent or being forced into the situation? Who justified the cause of the conspirators? Have any shown themselves as out and out blackguards? In such situations are people ever all good or all bad and how much are they affected by circumstances, conditions and so on? Is conspiracy ever justified? What does it feel like to be a conspirator?

ALTERNATIVES

Participants write, imagining themselves to be one of:

1	The escapees;	5	The climbers;
2	The survivors;	6	The prisoners;
3	The heroes;	7	The followers;
4	The refugees;	8	The prowlers.

COMMENT

An endless number of alternatives can be used to stimulate the imagination and explore situations.

CONVERSATIONS

PROCEDURE

Participants imagine themselves meeting a historical character. These might include Dick Turpin, Cleopatra, Martin Luther, Cromwell, George Washington, Marie Antoinette, Florence Nightingale, Joseph Stalin, Edgar Allan Poe or Shakespeare. They write down the conversation which would take place, bearing in mind what the historical characters did in life and why they are remembered.

DISCUSSION

How do members think the characters saw themselves and were seen by the public then, compared with the way we see and judge them today? Is our judgement any more true, or is it just a different viewpoint?

ALTERNATIVES

1　Each member writes, imagining someone from the future is having a conversation with them, giving some idea of how that person might see and view the member's life.
2　Participants write down a conversation which might occur on meeting an admired famous person.
3　This time each person imagines a conversation with someone famous with whom they disagree or whom they dislike.
4　Which fictional character would each member like to meet and what conversation would ensue?

COMMENT

These exercises can be written as short plays. It sometimes helps for participants to imagine that some incident is happening when the meeting takes place: perhaps a big occasion in the famous person's life. For other alternatives see *Historical Farce*, p58.

DOORS

PROCEDURE

Each person imagines that they have woken up in an empty room. They do not know where they are or how they got there. There is only one door. They open it and describe what they discover, what happens and how they feel about it. They can make it realistic, romantic, an Alice in Wonderland fantasy or anything else they please.

DISCUSSION

How willing is each person to take risks by exploring and building upon the situation? What fears or inhibitions stopped, or limited, the exploration of the world outside the door? Are these fears related to real life? Have group members help each other by suggesting ways to expand and explore each person's individual world, both imagined and real.

ALTERNATIVES

1 The door leads out of a garden; the participant has never been beyond its walls before.
2 The participant wakes up in a dark forest and follows a path out into daylight, open spaces and . . .
3 The door, this time, is a symbolic one and can be the door to:

   a) the imagination;   e) a different way of life;
   b) an ambition;   f) peace of mind;
   c) success;   g) happiness;
   d) a wish coming true;   h) fame.

COMMENT

Doing a few relaxation exercises before starting often helps members into the right frame of mind to begin this activity.

GROWING

PROCEDURE

Cut pictures of flowers, shrubs and trees from magazines and spread them around the room. Ask members to choose a picture and write the story of how the plant, or whatever it might be, grew from being a seed or cutting into the healthy growth in the picture. Suggest each person considers:

a) what difficulties the plant has had to overcome;

b) what pleasures and nourishment it derives from the world;

c) what pleasures and benefits it gives to the world.

If members feel comfortable with the idea, have them tell the story as if they are the plant.

DISCUSSION

Compare ideas on the process of growing. What problems have plants in common with humans regarding the struggle to survive, adapting to the environment, changing, being torn up and replanted elsewhere and so on?

ALTERNATIVES

Participants write as:

1 An animal being born and growing up;

2 An egg hatching and becoming a mature bird;

3 An idea being created, developed and brought to fruition.

COMMENT

These are good sources of inspiration for poetry. After doing the above exercise, have everyone work together to write a poem on the subject of growth.

PROBLEM AND OBJECTIVE

PROCEDURE

In this exercise a problem and objective are given. The participants imagine that they have been kidnapped and placed on an island. If they do not escape to the mainland, cross a desert and steal an aeroplane to fly back home by three o'clock on Saturday, their intended is going to marry someone else. Each person tells the story of the ordeal and how the objective is achieved, describing the emotions, physical hardships and so on.

DISCUSSION

Was it difficult to imagine the shock of being kidnapped and getting into this impossible situation? Talk about the way each person solved the various problems. Did some people meet the difficulties with a sense of humour? Can this attitude help with everyday problems? Could anyone imagine themselves courageous enough to do what they have written? What qualities make it possible to conquer seemingly impossible situations?

ALTERNATIVES

1 The participants imagine that they are carrying a drug to save someone's life, when their plane crash-lands in a jungle. They must get the drug to its destination within forty-eight hours.
2 Make each participant a secret agent who possesses information which could save life back in their own country. They have been betrayed and are surrounded by police. They must return to their own country within twelve hours for the information to be of any use.
3 Make it the type of problem that the participant might meet in everyday life.

COMMENT

It is best if you provide at least two or three obstacles between the problem and the objective. A useful problem-solving exercise.

A DIFFERENT PERSPECTIVE

PROCEDURE

Have everyone imagine that they are a small animal or insect. They could choose, for example, to be a rabbit, a cat, a snail, a worm, a cockroach, a bee or a hedgehog. They now write, describing an hour or a day in the chosen animal's or insect's life and how it might see its surroundings and humans. Ask people to describe the size of things and human behaviour towards the selected creature. Is it frightened or anxious? Does it hate or love humans?

DISCUSSION

How difficult is it to appreciate the viewpoint of something small? How does size affect the creature's life and the way it is treated? What does this tell us about ourselves and our natures?

ALTERNATIVES

1   Have group members imagine themselves as a large animal or some species bigger and more powerful than a human, such as an elephant, a giraffe, a hippopotamus, a whale, a shark or a crocodile.
2   This time ask everyone to write as a bird.
3   Imagine being a fish, with the ocean or a river as home.

COMMENT

For the results to be really effective, group members should avoid writing about the animals or humans in a sentimental fashion.

STORY-LINE

PROCEDURE

Prepare a number of situations for story beginnings equal to the number of people in the group, or have members make them up. Each individual writes down one of these beginnings — allow about five minutes. Stories are now passed on to the next person who continues the story-line. After another five minutes each story is passed on again. This continues until each person has written something on each story, the last five minutes bringing the tale to an end.

DISCUSSION

Discuss the ways people interpreted the various stories and how emphasis shifted. Did the story-lines turn out as each person had envisaged from what they wrote? If not, how had it been imagined that the stories would develop?

ALTERNATIVES

1 Stipulate that the stories must be romantic or humorous, stories of horror, adventure or mystery, science fiction and so on.
2 Call out a different category each time the stories are passed on.
3 Have each person write the complete story but change categories every five minutes and see how the story-lines are affected.

COMMENT

A light and entertaining exercise which demonstrates how change of emphasis or purpose alters the way things are viewed and the consequent outcome of events.

DISASTER

PROCEDURE

There has been a disaster. It could be a real disaster in which the participants have been involved or which they have read about, such as an accident, the loss of something valuable, a flood, a mining disaster, a ship sunk, a fire or it could be an imaginary disaster. Members write their experience of what happened as surviving victims, explaining how they felt.

DISCUSSION

What does facing disaster feel like? Exchange experiences of disasters. What happened afterwards? How did people manage? How does it feel, looking back on disaster? Did anything good or positive come out of it?

ALTERNATIVES

1   Write about the disaster in a reporter's style, examining the facts and giving an explanation for what happened.

2   Compose a poem commemorating the event.

3   Have members write a short sketch or play showing a confrontation between the company or person responsible for the disaster, and a surviving relative.

4   Participants write about the disaster, imagining themselves as being responsible for the accident or loss.

COMMENT

Have the individuals within the group work on different alternatives, examining different viewpoints. Or do a series of sessions and tackle them one at a time. Variations like the poem and play can be done as a group, with everyone working together, if desired.

OBSESSIONS

PROCEDURE

Make a list of absurd or harmless obsessions, such as giving love-bites, tearing up paper, fear of anything made of metal or wood, stroking hair, saying 'I love you' to every third person met, wearing silk next to your skin, opening windows, closing windows and so on. Ask group members to imagine themselves with one of these obsessions and to write about a ridiculous situation in which the habit has placed them. How did they feel having the obsession? How do they explain their way out of the situation?

DISCUSSION

Read out and discuss the ways in which obsessions can affect thought, word and motivation. When does an obsession become a problem? When is it a help?

ALTERNATIVES

Each participant writes about:

1 An obsession once experienced or one which they have now. This can be a simple habit like checking and rechecking doors that are locked, or nail-biting.
2 An obsession which can be given a positive direction to lead to success. This could be an overwhelming desire to be top at something like a sport, a hobby, a job and so on.

COMMENT

A really good interaction exercise. Everyone seems to enjoy trotting out personal and hated obsessions.

PROVERBS

PROCEDURE

Group members think of a proverb. Alternatively, supply a list and ask them to write a short incident or story which demonstrates the meaning of a chosen proverb. This can be a true story or an imagined one.

DISCUSSION

Is understanding of the proverbs made any more clear or real, or expanded by these stories? Can the same principle be used to explain other abstract ideas or widen understanding of feelings and emotions?

ALTERNATIVES

1   Write a story or relate an incident which explains an idea or moral. Examples are: men are chauvinistic, dogs are friends for life, cats are independent, first love is never forgotten and so on.

2   Write a story or recount an incident which demonstrates someone's feelings or emotions. Examples might be love, hate, jealousy or pride.

3   Cut out interesting pictures from magazines. Ask each person to write a paragraph expressing an idea or emotion which they think is represented by an individual picture.

4   Use quotations as the basis for a story or incident.

COMMENT

Use farcical or absurd statements to make this hilarious. Alternatively, have participants make up nonsense or wildly romantic stories to demonstrate the ideas.

STICKY SITUATIONS

PROCEDURE

Writers imagine that they are doctors with five patients. All are critically ill and the doctors have medicine to save only one person. They tell their patients and listen to the arguments each person puts forward to be saved. This can be written as a story, giving some description of each person and what is said, or as a play. Whichever form is used, the story must end with the doctor making his decision and giving his reasons.

DISCUSSION

Do the writers choose people to be saved who have the same attributes as themselves or those which they admire? Is this being fair and impartial? What moral problems have to be faced by the doctor? Compare the decisions each writer has made and ask other group members if they would have chosen the same person to survive. If not, why not?

ALTERNATIVES

1   Change the disaster situation to a doomed aeroplane with one parachute, a submarine with one frogman's suit, a spaceship with one spacesuit, a sinking boat with one life-jacket and so on.
2   Make the characters famous people such as politicians or film stars.
3   Form groups of six people. Individuals now write their own part in a play and argue for their own survival; or have them pretend to be famous people.

COMMENT

To ensure that this exercise has a light tone, have everyone think of it as a farce, exaggerating everything to the point of absurdity and putting up ridiculous arguments.

STORY ENDINGS

PROCEDURE

Present the participants with part or all of the last sentence in a story, article or poem. Each person writes a piece in his chosen form — story, article and so on — ending with the given sentence. Give members just the one sentence or, alternatively, provide a selection from whcih they can choose. Examples are:

a)   . . . fake or not, it was impossible to say.

b)   My happiness was assured!

c)   It was a case of winner takes all.

d)   This time I had come up to expectations.

e)   . . . fear had gone for good.

DISCUSSION

Encourage members to comment and suggest ways of improving the story, incident or poem. Has any member used personal experience to elaborate upon? If so, allow other group members to share similar experiences.

ALTERNATIVES

1   Present the participants with the climax of a story and have them write from the point when the problem began. They relate how the person in the story got into the situation, then how the difficulty was overcome. Either make up the situations or use ideas from popular stories.

2   Each person describes the events in someone's life, which might have made them into what they have become — a tramp, a thief, a hero, a romantic and so on. If you choose a negative character as the subject, have members finish by describing how the person could deflect the course of their life into more positive channels.

3   Participants describe the events and influences in life which have made them into the person they are at present. To avoid anyone presenting themselves as a negative person, have each member end by writing about possible steps they could take to change the course of their life — if necessary.

COMMENT

Sometimes, with problems, working back from the present enables us to get a different perspective and see various solutions. It is a method sometimes used by authors when writing twist-ending stories. Bear in mind that some people might find writing to a given ending difficult.

SURPRISE

PROCEDURE

Group members imagine themselves either jogging or walking in the country or a park when, suddenly, something amusing happens. Participants describe the time of day, their surroundings and what it is that happens. Give plenty of scope for exaggeration.

DISCUSSION

Did members imagine themselves being drawn into the incident or did they remain observers? Is this what usually happens to them in real life? How important is it to become involved? What are the fears of becoming involved?

ALTERNATIVES

Participants imagine and write about themselves:

1   Going about their daily business when they observe something puzzling. They describe what happens and how they react to it.
2   Travelling by car, in a train, or perhaps they are outdoors doing something when, suddenly, strange noises are heard. They become very curious. Participants describe what happens next.
3   Sitting at home late one evening, they are frightened by something which, afterwards, turns out to be a prank or a false alarm. They describe their initial reactions and how they might feel afterwards.

COMMENT

Use this exercise to enable participants to weave imaginative stories, or as an exercise to help them find out about themselves.

MODERN FAIRY-TALES

PROCEDURE

Read out or discuss a fairy-tale which has a hero, a heroine and a villain. Outline one or two popular modern stories or films which follow the same pattern. There is the good guy, the bad guy and the heroine in distress. Many mystery, cowboy and romantic stories provide examples.

Having made the participants aware of the pattern, ask them to write their own modern fairy-tale, setting it in their own town or locality. They can either use people they know, who might fall into the roles, or create their own characters. The story need not be a great adventure but could, for instance, be the simple story of a hero going to the rescue of a heroine who is in trouble with a villain pestering her at a party.

DISCUSSION

Have group members comment, with the aim of strengthening the story-lines. Have any members found themselves playing any of these roles in real life? Share experiences.

ALTERNATIVES

Have participants set their stories in:
1 A desert or jungle.
2 The American West. This can be before America was discovered or a later period.
3 The past. Select a historical period, discuss it for a few minutes, and then have everyone write.
4 The future. Select a time in the future and, before members begin to write, discuss what changes might have taken place.

COMMENT

There is good opportunity here for humour. This exercise is always good fun.

Exploring Relationships

CHOOSING FRIENDS

PROCEDURE

Everyone thinks about a present or past friend. They then describe the person, their qualities, what is liked about them and what benefits the participant derives from the relationship. These could include the confiding of emotional upsets, sharing of ideas, helping with the shopping or giving advice. Participants finish the exercise by writing what they feel they give to the relationship.

DISCUSSION

Have people picked friends with qualities similar to their own? What attracts a person in the selection of another for a friend? Discuss ideas on the qualities of a good friend and how participants themselves measure up to their own criteria.

ALTERNATIVES

Participants describe:

1 Someone disliked; they end by making a list of similar things disliked in themselves.
2 Someone admired. What qualities have they that the participants themselves would like?
3 An imaginary ideal friend. What qualities are those of the participants themselves? How many are attributes they would like to possess?
4 The qualities they think a friend would find in them.
5 How they imagine a person they dislike would see them. What qualities might this person see?

COMMENT

Have members describe several friends and their different qualities. Ask them to include the needs satisfied by each person.

FIRST IMPRESSIONS

PROCEDURE

Instruct group members to think about the last time they met someone new and whom they now know quite well. Have them write an account of that meeting, recording their first impressions of the person and how they felt during the meeting. Also, have them include how they see that person now and whether or not the first impression was a true one.

DISCUSSION

Were there any misleading images from the first impression? How did these influence getting to know the other person? Did the initial impression affect the emotional reaction to the person?

ALTERNATIVES

Members write:

1 Expressing the sort of impression they think they make on a first meeting.
2 Describing the type of impression they would like to give.
3 About the impression they try to give in different situations. This could be meeting a new girlfriend, someone disliked, a good friend, someone who can do them a favour, someone who wants a favour, a neighbour, family members, strangers, a prospective employer at a job interview and so on.
4 About the real person behind the impressions they seek to create when meeting other people.

COMMENT

It helps to give a specific situation so that members can envisage themselves creating an impression. Encourage the use of physical description.

BEHAVIOUR

PROCEDURE

Participants think back to their childhood, to an incident when they performed well at school, helped with a job at home, bought a gift for their parents or did something which they felt warranted praise or recognition. They describe what it was they did, what reaction it prompted from their parents and how it felt when and after it happened.

DISCUSSION

How important is being recognised for doing something special? Did what happened then influence the way participants feel and react in these situations now? Do members treat other people and their own family in the same way as they were treated? When was the last time members praised someone for doing something for them?

ALTERNATIVES

Each person writes about a childhood incident:
1 Recalling something they did wrong and for which they were criticised.
2 Describing what happened when they did something good, bad, or a combination of one followed by the other, to get attention.

COMMENT

This exercise works best when some trust has been built up between members of the group.

MAKING FRIENDS

PROCEDURE

Group members write the story of how they made one particular friend. They describe the friend, how they met, how the friendship developed and continued and what it means to them.

DISCUSSION

What are the difficulties about meeting people and making friends? Do members find it easy or difficult? What can participants teach each other from personal experience? How do people differ in approach and attitude, and how does this influence making friends? Why make friends at all?

ALTERNATIVES

Participants write about:

1   Their attitudes towards making friends. Do they prefer a lot or just a few friends? Do they mix easily or never feel accepted; perhaps stay aloof or prefer their own company? What rewards and responsibilities do friends bring?
2   Making friends with people of the same sex.
3   Making friends with people of the opposite sex.
4   Making friends with older people.
5   Making friends with younger people.

COMMENT

To explore the subject fully, these exercises are best done as a series — or have members write simultaneously on alternatives.

ROLE CHANGES

PROCEDURE

Participants describe what changes took place in life as they grew up and became young men or women. What attitudes changed? How did relationships with parents alter? What changes took place between brothers and sisters and how did the participants see them? What conflicts were there? How many of these were resolved? Do some still remain today?

If participants prefer, focus on one incident of change: leaving home, making one's own decisions, being given responsibility, not being approved of and so on.

DISCUSSION

Share experience of changes. Do any changes from a long time ago still affect life and family relationships today? Do members find adapting to change difficult? Exchange ideas on coping with change.

ALTERNATIVES

Participants describe the changes necessary:

1 As a parent with a child who is growing into a young man or woman;
2 When adapting from being single to living with someone or being married;
3 When adapting to being the parent of a new baby;
4 On becoming a grandparent;
5 On accepting that a parent's or child's viewpoint on life will be different from one's own;
6 On accepting that one's own life, owing to circumstances or opinion, has to be lived differently to that envisaged.

COMMENT

Role changes in life are many. More alternatives can be added to suit the ages and needs of the group.

BEING RESPONSIBLE

PROCEDURE

Ask participants to recall and write about an occasion in their lives when they have had to be in charge of someone or something. This responsibility could be for escorting an elderly person across the road, for a junior employee, or for the care of a friend's prized possession. Participants describe how they came to be given the responsibility, how they reacted to it and the outcome.

DISCUSSION

How does it feel to be in charge? Do members respond in different ways, some feeling comfortable and others uncomfortable in this role? Does having the responsibility affect how each person reacts to situations? Does it affect whether or not they become involved in events?

ALTERNATIVES

Have members write about themselves as:

1 A policeman who has been called to the assistance of an elderly lady. She has been robbed and is in a hysterical state.
2 An air hostess in charge of a frightened passenger.
3 A nurse in charge of a patient who is frightened of having an operation.
4 A person who has found a lost child.
5 A teenager in charge of an elderly grandparent who is confused.

COMMENT

Many more situations can be thought up to suit the ages and life-styles of participants. Also, have members write, imagining themselves as the person who is being helped. This time, discuss views on trusting someone else in these circumstances.

VISITS

PROCEDURE

Group members name the district or area in which they live and give a very brief verbal description of it. Participants then decide upon another member they would like to visit. They now write, first describing their own home, district, fears, hopes and preparations for the visit. Next they imagine the journey across town, what the area being visited is like and their feelings about going there to meet this person. Finally they write what happens during the imaginary visit, giving their reactions.

DISCUSSION

Share fears and experiences of meeting new people in unfamiliar surroundings. What are the rewards of overcoming problems and actually doing this? How accurate is the participants' perception of the visit compared with their host's?

ALTERNATIVES

Members write imagining themselves:

1   As the host.
2   Either visiting or being host to a pen-friend from a different country.
3   Either visiting or being host to someone from a different cultural origin.

COMMENT

This exercise allows members to compare their expectations and fears with those of the proposed host, and vice versa. It can be helpful to the discussion to have some members writing as hosts, while others write as visitors.

SOCIAL SETTINGS

PROCEDURE

Participants write about going to a party which is attended by men and women of roughly the same age as themselves. They know one or two people vaguely. They describe arriving, how they feel and what they do at the party. Do they approach new people or head for one person whom they know and cling to that one person? Do they talk to people who speak to them, take part in any games and help themselves to food and drink? They describe what they feel and what they think about themselves and others at the party.

DISCUSSION

Compare the ways in which participants handle the situation and examine whether or not they use it to make new friends. What were the hindrances? How can these be overcome? Share feelings and anxieties.

ALTERNATIVES

Participants write about:

1 Mixing with colleagues and associates at work.

2 Going into a restaurant, pub or sports club.

3 Travelling on public transport.

4 Mixing at a party, or being at home with friends who have similar interests.

5 Inviting home people whom they do not know well and with whom they do not have many interests in common. They may be older, younger or people from a recently joined social group.

6 Going out with a husband, wife, friend or someone to whom the participant is sexually attracted.

COMMENT

Social settings can be invented to suit the needs of the group members. Try having them choose social settings with which they feel most comfortable or uncomfortable.

LISTENING

PROCEDURE

Have group members invent an incident in which two, three or four people are talking about something. Each person is trying to put over their own viewpoint and not listening to any of the others. Participants describe what happens. Do one or more of the people involved become tense, frustrated, disgusted, rude or walk away? How does the incident end?

DISCUSSION

Does this happen often in life? Have any of the participants taken part in a similar scene or been guilty of not listening? How does it feel to go away, aware that no one has been listening to you? How does it make participants view their friends or make friends feel about them?

ALTERNATIVES

1 Participants describe an incident when they have been guilty of not listening.
2 Each person writes about an occasion when someone did not listen to them.
3 Participants describe an incident within the family as in (1) or (2) above.
4 Form groups of two, three or four people and have each person write their own part in a short play.
5 Write a poem about listening, with each group member contributing something to it.

COMMENT

If anyone has difficulty getting started, give a topic for the characters in the incident to talk about. A personal problem, an emotional upset, or a strong conviction about something serves best.

HOSTILITIES

PROCEDURE

Members write the story of their lives, recalling it in terms of hostilities and tensions. What conflicts do they remember from childhood — between themselves and others, and between members of the family? Did these hostilities continue throughout their youth? Did other conflicts creep in? Which hostilities still occur?

DISCUSSION

Is there any connection between present and past hostilities? Have these tensions, conflicts and the rest influenced relationships? Have they become accepted handicaps, so that nothing is done about them?

ALTERNATIVES

Each person writes the story of their lives, recalling it in terms of:
1 Fears about relationships;
2 Things that offered security and stability in relationships;
3 Harmony and a sense of rapport discovered through relationships.

COMMENT

Write in the same manner about other topics. Examples could include hates, loves, likes, dislikes; things that have aroused anger or things that have given pleasure.

INTERACTION

PROCEDURE

Ask each person to assess how they interact with a member of the group — or several members — and write about it, bringing in emotional reaction. Some aspects for the writers to consider are whether they:

agree all the time	tell jokes
try to be helpful	ask for opinions
lead the conversation	listen
give advice	force their own opinions
evade questions	ignore some people
judge	offer ideas
criticise	help resolve problems
give information about themselves	withdraw
ask for information	resist interaction

DISCUSSION

Read out the pieces and see if other group members agree. Discuss the relevance of the above and any other points which apply to successful interaction.

ALTERNATIVES

Participants write about how they interact with:

1 Other members of their family;
2 Personal friends;
3 A group of strangers such as one might meet on a first visit to a club, class, society and so on;
4 Colleagues at work.

COMMENT

If group members are a little hesitant, start the session with a short discussion or have them introduce themselves.

THE FAMILY

PROCEDURE

Participants imagine that it is a beautiful day. They and their family are all together in the garden or a park. They write describing the family playing a game and include the reaction of every family member as he or she takes part. Who suggests and organises the game, who is reluctant and who is the enthusiastic one? How does each person perform? Who wins, and how does everyone feel afterwards?

DISCUSSION

Are group members happy with the role they played in the game? Did they feel comfortable, stifled or restricted? How would they like it to have been? Did they play out of duty or because they wanted to?

ALTERNATIVES

Each participant writes:
1 Describing a day out with the family.
2 Describing each member of the family doing something at home and how it is done in each case.
3 Imagining the family being homeless and having to put up a tent; describing the scene and how each person would react. Who would help, in which way?
4 Describing each member of the family reacting and solving an invented problem presented by the group leader.
5 Imagining the family in a made-up situation — one presented by the group leader, or one invented by the participant. They describe which role each family member plays. Who takes charge? Who solves problems? Who panics?

COMMENT

Being honest about family relationships in a group setting can be difficult for people who feel bound by duty and loyalty. Building a sense of trust within the group and giving plenty of reassurance about confidentiality helps.

OPPOSING VIEWS

PROCEDURE

Each person writes about a series of actions or incidents, both verbal and physical, involving two people with opposing views about something. The action can be between a boy and girl, man and wife, teacher and student, patient and nurse or an incident that the participant has experienced. Ask people to make clear at the outset of their story what the conflict is and explain the difference of opinion. Next they should show how these difficulties are resolved. Do the opposing people part, still angry and resentful? Do they attempt to understand each other's viewpoints, or do they finish up physically assaulting each other?

DISCUSSION

If differences are not resolved in the narrative, talk about ways in which they might have been. Is it possible for two people to have different opinions and work or live together without coming to blows? Does this mean compromising? Should compromising be resisted? How much of the conflict in argument is due to people not listening?

ALTERNATIVES

Each participant writes about:
1 One man or woman opposing a group of people;
2 One man or woman's struggle against an official body such as a council, committee or society;
3 One person resisting an idea: a company policy, a new law, an ideal, a principle and so on.

COMMENT

Dealing with minor conflicts and opposing forces is part of the pressure of everyday living. Once people get going, this can be a good exercise for letting off steam, as well as dealing with relationships.

ATTITUDES

PROCEDURE

Each person thinks back to an attitude once held and which has since changed. They may have felt bitter or angry about something or someone. This has now — perhaps because of changed circumstances — turned to sympathy, sorrow or love. They write, stating the initial attitude, how and why it changed and what it is now. Also they should include the ways in which this change of attitude has influenced relationships.

DISCUSSION

Can attitudes alter relationships and change ability to make and keep friends? Discuss the way attitudes have affected members' lives.

ALTERNATIVES

Participants write about:

1 The attitudes of others towards them and their own way of living; how these have changed relationships and the direction of their lives.
2 Their attitudes towards officials: police, politicians, traffic wardens, social workers, ticket collectors, meter-readers, postmen and so on. Are the attitudes directed at the official capacity or the person?
3 Attitudes towards life in general.
4 Attitudes towards other members of their family.
5 An attitude they have which they would like to change. They describe how they would like it to influence their relationships with others.

COMMENT

Some people find it difficult to think of attitudes, especially their own. Often a list on a board or having members call out different attitudes can get the thought process started.

SUPPRESSED WORDS

PROCEDURE

In this exercise, request that participants think back to their childhood or teens and write about the things they were not allowed to say or express feelings about at home. These are things which remain unspoken and may include not telling someone they were loved or disliked, expressing hurt at an incident, having to do something not understood, avoiding discussion of unpleasant or taboo subjects and so on.

DISCUSSION

Talk about the difference between what participants felt they could say and what they wanted to say. How did this affect them at the time, and their attitudes and relationships since?

ALTERNATIVES

Each person writes in the same manner about:

1　Things which remain unexpressed in various relationships they have had throughout life, for example, with brothers, sisters, friends, husband or wife or workmates.
2　Things they were not allowed to do.

COMMENT

This can sometimes be a difficult exercise to get going, but do not avoid it as it can be particularly rewarding. It can give people more understanding of how they communicate and use language and why they have difficulty making others understand them. To make it easier, suggest that everyone writes down the first thing that comes into their head.

BODY LANGUAGE

PROCEDURE

Describe a friend, revealing how he or she expresses their state of mind, attitudes and desires through body language. Bear in mind:

facial expression	use of body space
posture	touching
hand gestures	stance
eye movement	mannerisms

DISCUSSION

How does body language influence communication? Is it necessary to use it in the right way in order to be understood and to understand others? Discuss how each member of the group uses body language and how it is interpreted by the others.

ALTERNATIVES

Each person writes about:

1   Meeting someone they want to impress. They describe the body language used by both parties.

2   Meeting a friend who needs consoling because of some misfortune. They include what they would look for which might indicate the friend's state of mind and help them to respond.

3   Being at a party where they meet new people. They describe the body language they would use to get across to some that they are interested in advancing friendship; then the body language used to indicate rejection of others.

4   An incident with two or more people which shows tension and aggression.

5   The body language used in order to negotiate a settlement with someone disliked. They describe which signals and reactions would occur during the incident.

COMMENT

Many more situations can be invented to suit the requirements of the participants.

COMMUNICATION

PROCEDURE

Group members imagine themselves at home among the people with whom they feel most comfortable and whom they trust. They write a few paragraphs describing the scene and how it feels emotionally. They include any conversation which ensues. It might be helpful to give a theme: something active like making or eating a meal while discussing something important. When this has been completed get the group to rewrite the same conversation imagining themselves in a different environment with different people — perhaps at work with an employer, on a train with a stranger or in a pub talking to someone disliked. Again, encourage them to record emotions.

DISCUSSION

How has the change of scene and people affected the writer's ability to communicate the same conversation? Are the same words used? Is the same information given? Does any restriction of what is said influence the ability to communicate accurately what is truly felt? Do both parties understand the same thing from what is said?

ALTERNATIVES

Each person writes:
1 About a personal or emotional problem as if telling it to a best friend. They then rewrite, explaining the same problem to a solicitor, employer, benefits clerk or someone they hardly know.
2 Explaining something which will be a disappointment to someone they do not want to hurt or offend. They then rewrite, giving the same information to someone disliked.

COMMENT

Every day we edit and change information about the way we feel, giving different versions to people — and sometimes wrong impressions. For other exercises, concentrating mainly on communicating facts and physical events, see *Interpretations*, p35.

FAMILY VIEWPOINTS

PROCEDURE

Everyone writes about how they perceive their relationship with other members of their families. Is it good, bad, distant, perhaps impossible with one person? Do two or more in the family gang up together? Is the participant approved of by others in the family? Does the participant approve of them? Ask members to think of, or try to invent, an incident to illustrate the relationships.

DISCUSSION

Share experiences and feelings. Also encourage comments, reaction and the airing of other viewpoints by group members.

ALTERNATIVES

Participants write:

1 About an incident, showing how they see themselves as a parent, son or daughter.
2 Imagining an incident which shows how they would like to be as a parent, son or daughter.
3 About an incident which shows their child, father or mother as they see them.
4 About an incident showing their child, father or mother as they would like them to be.
5 Showing how every member of the family see themselves and the participant.
6 Showing how each member of the family would like them to be.
7 Expressing opinions on the way in which other family members' viewpoints on life differ from their own. What goals in life are different?

COMMENT

These are good exercises for enabling members to share experience and understand other viewpoints within the family.

MANIPULATION

PROCEDURE

Instruct participants to think back to an occasion when they believed they were being manipulated or used by a friend or acquaintance. Each member writes an account of the incident, recalling their impression of the person and how they felt about the offender before, during and after the event. Was the aim of the manipulator good or bad?

DISCUSSION

Share experiences. Does living with someone mean manipulating another person both for selfish and genuine purposes? How far is it permissible to go in manipulating someone else? Or is it completely out of the question?

ALTERNATIVES

Participants describe an incident when:

1   They manipulated a friend or acquaintance;
2   A family member manipulated them;
3   They manipulated a family member.

COMMENT

Use similar exercises to explore individual experiences of being manipulated by social, political and group forces.

CHILDHOOD MEMORIES

PROCEDURE

Participants describe themselves as children and their relationship within the family. If possible, they recall an incident to demonstrate this. Have them include physical appearance, setting, how they felt about their parents and how they think they themselves were seen. Were they favoured, the odd one out, kept at a distance, or what?

DISCUSSION

Share memories and experiences. Do they — or would they — treat their own children in that way? Does the way relationships were experienced and learned within the family affect the way they relate to friends now?

ALTERNATIVES

Participants describe:

1　Themselves and their parents as they would have liked the relationship to be.
2　An imaginary family history. If they could have chosen their own parents, family history and background, what would that choice have been?
3　A happy childhood memory.
4　A childhood incident which caused personal unhappiness or frustration.
5　The first friend remembered as a child.
6　The first person disliked as a child and what happened to make the participant dislike them.

COMMENT

Sometimes people need prompting to recall early memories. Stimulate by having a short discussion before beginning to write.

MASTER AND SERVANT

PROCEDURE

Taking either a realistic or a romantic approach, participants imagine themselves to be a master who has a servant to look after all his needs. They describe the scene as they give the servant tasks to carry out and how they feel while doing this. Then ask everyone to change roles and write about how it feels to be the servant doing the tasks.

DISCUSSION

Did members find it easier to be master or servant? Did they feel any different about what they had written as master after writing as servant? Does putting yourself in another person's place help you to understand how that person feels? What effect does understanding have on the way you treat and relate to others?

ALTERNATIVES

1   Make the servant disliked by the master and then make him likeable. Does this alter the relationship?
2   Instead of master and servant, make the relationship one of the following:

nurse and patient	stewardess and passenger
employer and employee	instructor and pupil
landlord and tenant	money-collector and debtor
sergeant and private	warder and prisoner

COMMENT

Many more master-and-servant situations can be added. Make them applicable to the participants' lifestyle.

FIRST MEETINGS

PROCEDURE

Ask group members to imagine meeting and making a new friend. What recent experience would they like to share with this person? Have everyone describe an incident during which they make a new friend and share this experience.

DISCUSSION

Encourage members to talk about the type of experiences they share with friends. What information would they not discuss with someone new but perhaps share with someone known and trusted? Are there any topics they would not share, even with a trusted friend? Why not?

ALTERNATIVES

Each participant imagines and writes about sharing an experience with:

1　A prospective boyfriend or girlfriend;
2　Someone who lives next door;
3　An unknown person who has just arrived from another country;
4　A person who has very different cultural origins;
5　A being from outer space on a first visit to earth.

COMMENT

Have members select one of the above alternatives and relate an imagined personal experience they would like that person to share with them. Also invent other alternatives to suit the needs of the group.

THANK YOU

PROCEDURE

Each person writes a letter to a friend thanking them for a kindness, an invitation or present. They tell the recipient how the kindness, or whatever it might be, has helped, how it is appreciated, and what having them as a friend means.

DISCUSSION

Why write a thank-you letter? How does it feel to do something for someone and then not hear the result of your kindness? How does receiving a thank-you letter make the recipient feel towards the sender? Should friends know how we feel about them? When was the last time group members told a friend how they felt about them?

ALTERNATIVES

Participants write thank-you letters to:

1 A professional or business person such as a solicitor, doctor or builder for good service.

2 Someone who has sorted out a complaint and seen the participant has had fair redress.

3 A member of the family — son, daughter, husband, wife, grandparent — from whom the participant is temporarily separated, saying how and why they are missed.

4 Someone previously unknown who has returned something of value which was lost or stolen.

5 Another group member for a kindness or good turn the writer imagines that person could do.

COMMENT

Having group members send each other thank-you letters promotes good feelings in the group and allows them to experience praise.

FILLING A SPACE

PROCEDURE

Group members study the group and choose someone who could have been a member of their family — or a friend who, had he or she existed, would have filled a space in the participant's life. It might be a son, daughter, brother, sister, business partner, companion, someone to confide in and so on. Now ask each participant to write about the space that person would have filled.

DISCUSSION

After each reading let members try to guess who represents the space in the author's life. Encourage those who have experienced what the author desires to share their good fortune.

ALTERNATIVES

Members describe:

1 An ordinary living person whom they would like to know and who would fill a space in their life. This could be someone at work or someone seen when out socially. Members write down why they want to know this person and what he or she would add to their lives.

2 A person they admire who is famous; they write about the new dimension that person would add to their life.

COMMENT

An exercise which gives a warm feeling and a boost to the ego of the person selected to fill the space.

INHERITANCE

PROCEDURE

In this exercise participants describe a characteristic inherited and how it has affected their lives and relationships. How did it show itself and affect the relationship with the person from whom it was inherited? Examples might include poor eyesight, short temper, good looks, easy-going nature, optimism, sense of fairness, meanness or athletic ability.

DISCUSSION

How much are we affected by inherited temperament and traits? How much is learned from other members of the family and can the trait — if undesirable — be changed? How much control has the individual over what he or she is?

ALTERNATIVES

Members write about:
1 The traits they would like to have inherited and what difference they would make to their life.
2 The traits they would like their children to inherit from them, giving the reasons why.
3 An object they have inherited, telling what they have done, or intend to do, with it, what it means to them and how their intentions might differ from that envisaged by the benefactor.
4 Any objects they would like to inherit in the future, giving the reasons why.
5 Any objects they would like their children to inherit from them, giving the reasons why.

COMMENT

Start the group off by having members write a list of traits on a board or a sheet of paper.

SPEAKING OUT

PROCEDURE

Group members envisage themselves being opposite two strangers. This can be on a bus, in an aeroplane, in a cafe or in the park. The strangers are talking loudly, exercising opinions which the participant considers boring, pretentious and stupid, eventually being moved to interrupt, saying, "Rubbish!" Members write, describing the event and what happens next.

DISCUSSION

Ask members whether they would interrupt in real life. If not, why not? Discuss the reasons: shyness, convention, social position, rudeness, private thoughts better kept to oneself, consideration of other people's feelings and so on. When might interrupting be appropriate?

ALTERNATIVES

Each person writes about:
1   An occasion, outside the family, when they would like to have spoken out and did not. They imagine what would have happened if they had and describe it.
2   A family incident when they felt they could listen no longer to a parent, son or daughter. What was the outcome?
3   Any subject about which they have kept quiet, never daring to speak out. This could be an opinion, a criticism of a person, a criticism of an idea, an attitude they did not like and so on.

COMMENT

If group members wish, allow them to write a poem around the subject, or have the group compose a poem. Alternatively, divide everyone into groups of three, with each person writing their own part in a short play.

MAKING DECISIONS

PROCEDURE

A member of the family or a friend is coming to visit for a day. Participants have to decide what food to prepare for them and how to entertain the visitor. This can be an actual person who has visited or might visit, or an imaginary person. Participants describe the visit, saying what the guest's fads and fancies are, what is planned, the person's reaction to it all, and how it feels to make the decisions, during and after the event.

DISCUSSION

What are the difficulties and responsibilities of making decisions in this way? Compare reactions and ways of coping. Does anyone go to extremes to avoid this kind of arrangement? How does it feel to have made someone's visit a success? How do participants react to having a visit planned for them?

ALTERNATIVES

Participants write:

1 Describing a journey or holiday they have arranged, and which was shared with a friend. This can be real or imagined.
2 Imagining themselves being left in charge of a friend's house. A water tank bursts, causing extensive damage. They have to sort out the repair work to the house and all the personal effects.
3 Imagining they are looking after a neighbour's pet animal when an accident occurs to it; describing how it feels making the decisions for the animal's welfare.
4 Imagining they have been given a once-in-a-lifetime chance. It will change the whole way of life for their family or a friend and means moving house. They describe the process of coming to a decision.

COMMENT

Invent fantasy, adventure, unlikely events or situations in which group members could find themselves with friends or members of their families. Also, turn the situation around: have participants write about how it feels to have someone else making decisions for them.

107

DISAPPOINTMENT

PROCEDURE

Group members write about going to a party, to which they have been looking forward and which they have taken a great deal of trouble to attend. They arrive to be informed by a distressed host that the party has been cancelled and are told to go home. Ask each member to include in their account how they felt before arriving, what their reaction was on hearing the news, what they did or said next and how they felt about it afterwards.

DISCUSSION

Who reacted angrily? Were any members concerned only about themselves? Who wrote about the host or why the cancellation happened? Can any members give reasons why they reacted in the way they did? Compare different reactions and ways of handling the situation.

ALTERNATIVES

1   Write the above or a similiar experience from the viewpoint of the host who has cancelled the party.
2   Write about not receiving an expected birthday present.
3   This time the writer has forgotten to buy someone a present.
4   Someone the participant depends upon has let them down. Have them write about it.
5   Lastly, each person writes about letting someone down who depends upon them.

COMMENT

Many more alternatives can be added. It is sometimes a good idea to have half the group write expressing the experience of being disappointed and the other half the experience of disappointing others. Or use one viewpoint in one session and another in a future session.

RISKS

PROCEDURE

Each person writes about the risk element in making a new friend. They consider rejection, hurt, disappointment, commitment, giving, receiving and sharing information. Also, having to adapt to what others want to do, persuading another to do what they want or coping with any conflicts of interest. They describe their attitude and feeling about taking the above and other risks. Have them include the rewards that are achieved by taking reasonable risks. Examples: sharing good times, having someone to talk to, having someone to help when necessary, companionship and so on.

DISCUSSION

Compare attitudes of group members. Are the rewards of having friends and being involved with the family worth taking the risks for? Is the price of loneliness too great if you do not take them? Will participants risk saying 'no' sometimes after deciding that a friend's suggestions are not for them? Which risks are unreasonable and should not be taken?

ALTERNATIVES

Participants write about:

1   Meeting a new person, opening a conversation, having to accept or reject an offer for coffee and also to decide upon a further commitment. Do they meet the risks with anxiety or pleasure?

2   The risk elements in an incident with someone of the opposite sex. This person is obviously attracted to the participant who quite likes him or her, but is not interested in a serious relationship.

3   Becoming involved in a group, society, club or class in which they will be expected to take part. They highlight the risks and the rewards.

4   An incident in which their car has broken down or something else has gone wrong. They have to find and ask someone for help. They highlight the risks and the successful outcome.

5   The risks of being involved in family affairs. They conclude by stating the benefits.

COMMENT

Apply the exercise to any risk-taking situation: changing jobs, a new and expensive hobby, moving accommodation, going on a journey, a day out, going shopping in the rush hour, going out after dark.

Developing Awareness

A DAY IN THE LIFE

PROCEDURE

Participants write about a recent, typical day in their lives. They start by describing waking up, getting out of bed, thoughts and impressions of the morning and attitudes towards what the day holds. They then describe the day, the people they met, the jobs and activities accomplished, ending with going to bed again and their last thoughts for the day.

DISCUSSION

Has anyone examined their day in this way before? Are they surprised, pleased or dissatisfied with it? Has anyone discovered anything about themselves of which they were unaware? How do we go about altering what is scheduled to happen during a day if we want to change it? Compare methods of organising and getting mundane, everyday things done.

ALTERNATIVES

Participants describe:
1   A day remembered from childhood;
2   A day experienced five or ten years ago;
3   A day as they would like it to be now;
4   A day as they would like it to be in the future.

COMMENT

Stopping to think how we spend time can be an eye-opener.

GRAFFITI

PROCEDURE

Instruct participants to write a few pages of graffiti about all the things in themselves which they do not like and think should be changed. These can be small, irritating facets which bother them — being forgetful, having a condescending attitude, and so on.

DISCUSSION

Has anyone learned anything about themselves which they did not know before? How do the things written about affect the way participants see themselves? Do other members agree? Discuss ways of changing.

ALTERNATIVES

Participants write graffiti about:
1   Colleagues at work;
2   People in authority;
3   Other family members;
4   Friends and neighbours.

COMMENT

Instead of writing disparaging graffiti, have participants write an appreciation of themselves, colleagues at work and so on.

LEAVING AND ARRIVING

PROCEDURE

How often have participants left one place and moved on to another? Examples might include moving house, leaving a place of work to go home, home to go on holiday, one town for another, one county to live in another, hospital to go home. Everyone describes their feelings on leaving and the change in emotions which take place as they arrive at their destination.

DISCUSSION

Share emotive experiences. Who feels most strongly pulled back to the place left and who is eager to experience new places? What makes each person feel the way they do? Does writing and talking about the experience tell anyone anything about themselves? Can other group members comment on what is revealed about each person?

ALTERNATIVES

Participants describe:

1 How it feels having to leave one or several people because of circumstances and going on to meet and make a new friend or friends.

2 Leaving one experience and going on to another. Examples: being dependent on someone, then becoming independent; working for someone, then being your own boss; working on shifts, then normal hours; changing from being single to being married; being employed and then unemployed and so on.

COMMENT

'Leaving and arriving' exercises serve well to inspire verse and poetry.

GOOD TURNS

PROCEDURE

Ask group members to think about some task they have performed successfully for someone. Examples might include cooking a meal, decorating a room, knitting a jumper, weeding the garden, baking a cake or doing an errand. Participants write about it, how they felt as they worked and the feeling when they had completed the task. Also have them include:

a) how they thought of themselves afterwards;

b) how they assessed the other person's views of them afterwards.

DISCUSSION

Did doing something successfully for someone else change or reinforce anyone's opinion of themself? Did it change the way the other person reacted to them? In what way? How important is it to set tasks and targets which can be completed successfully?

ALTERNATIVES

Participants write about success with:

1 Selecting, buying and giving someone a present.

2 Doing something they enjoy with another person: going to the theatre, for a walk, fishing, dancing, singing, sewing and so on.

3 Making a difficult decision involving other people. This may be refusing to do something against their principles or simply because they did not want to do it.

COMMENT

These exercises help participants to promote a more positive image of themselves.

POSITIVE AND NEGATIVE

PROCEDURE

Ask participants to consider their own character. What are their good points? Are they determined, good-looking, loyal, a good cook, helpful to others, kind, etc? Then have them contemplate their dislikes, weaknesses and failings. They write about:

a)   the positive side of their character,

b)   the negative side of their character.

DISCUSSION

Are any weaknesses expressed by some members considered to be strengths by others? Do the rest of the group see each person as that person sees himself or herself? Which characteristic in themselves would each member like to change?

ALTERNATIVES

Members write, describing:

1   The characteristics in themselves which they would like to keep and those they would like to change;

2   What each considers to be his real self, then his ideal self;

3   Changes they must make in their characters to achieve the goals set in life.

COMMENT

In some groups it may be prudent to ensure a positive outcome. This can be done by stipulating that participants write about at least one positive characteristic for each negative one described.

MOUNTAIN

PROCEDURE

Have people write, portraying themselves as a mountain. Ask them to consider where the mountain is located, what plantation and animal life it supports, who lives on it and so on. Also have each person include the way their characteristics show up in the shape and type of terrain.

DISCUSSION

Have each piece read out anonymously and see if the authors can be identified. Is each mountain as other members of the group imagined it would be? How would members visiting other mountains find them: pleasant, mysterious, interesting or unfriendly?

ALTERNATIVES

Participants write, portraying themselves as:

1 A storm;
2 A fire;
3 A wind;
4 A waterfall;
5 A stream;
6 A lake or ocean;
7 A wave;
8 A volcano.

COMMENT

Many more variations of a similar nature can be added. The exercise can also be followed up by having members describe a day spent visiting someone else's mountain, caught in someone else's storm, sailing on someone else's lake and so on.

LOOKING INTO THE FUTURE

PROCEDURE

Instruct group members to think about the sort of problems or difficulties they might personally encounter in the near or distant future. Ask them to write, describing one such problem, how they see themselves overcoming it, and the end result.

DISCUSSION

Can group members add other solutions to those read out by individuals? Talk about general problems everyone has to face: ageing, unforeseen events, health, changes in circumstances and so on. Do members of the group see themselves coping with and overcoming these changes?

ALTERNATIVES

Each person writes about:

1 A future problem within their family;
2 A future problem in their social life;
3 A physical problem they might have to face in the future;
4 A political problem which will alter their future and way of life.

COMMENT

To keep this a positive exercise, emphasise the solving of the problem each person writes about. Be sure to examine the variety of solutions offered by other group members.

BUILDINGS

PROCEDURE

Ask participants to imagine and write about themselves as a building. What sort of building is it? How many rooms does it have? Who or what is contained in it? What sort of character has it? Is it a pleasant, elegant, welcoming building, or is it stand-offish? Have everyone describe the building in detail, what goes on in it, and how it views the world.

DISCUSSION

How does it feel, pretending to be a building? Do other members of the group think the building is a true picture of the person, or does the person come across differently? Do buildings have living, breathing characters? If so, why?

ALTERNATIVES

1   Have participants describe objects, plants, landscapes, animals, dusks and dawns and so on in the same way.
2   Make the object, or whatever it might be, represent the way the participant feels.
3   Have the building, or whatever it might be, represent what the participant would most like to be.
4   This time make it represent what the participant would least like to be.

COMMENT

This exercise can help participants to take a more objective view of themselves. It also enables them to compare the way they see themselves with the way others see them, and aids their descriptive and appreciative powers. For fun, allow people to exaggerate their attributes to the point of absurdity.

APPRAISING PEOPLE

PROCEDURE

In this exercise people imagine something happening while the group is still together and write as if it has already happened. Request that:

a) names be mentioned;

b) short descriptions of people be given;

c) speech and actions of each person be reported.

DISCUSSION

Read out the pieces and let each person comment on the actions and views attributed to them. How accurate have participants been in assessing the reactions of others?

ALTERNATIVES

1   Each participant imagines what would happen if, because of a snowstorm, the group was trapped in the building overnight and the group leader was taken ill.

2   Give a subject to the group. Examples might include censorship, cruelty to animals, wildlife preservation, feminism, beauty contests or travel. Have each person write up a group debate.

3   Conjure up the bare bones of any situation or problem in which the group might be involved and have each person write the story of it. Each member of the group must feature in the event and the solution.

COMMENT

Try this exercise when the group members are unfamiliar with each other. Later, when they are better acquainted, do one of the alternatives. Compare and discuss the results of both sessions.

REPORTER

PROCEDURE

Participants imagine that they are a newspaper reporter sent to the scene of an accident at an accident black spot. The reporter has a reputation for presenting a highly personalised viewpoint. Participants invent causes and background to the accident and write the report to be published, expressing their own personal opinions in a forthright manner. They say who is responsible and state what should be done to prevent further accidents.

DISCUSSION

Read out and discuss participants' viewpoints. Focus on trying to make members appreciate and question alternative ways of looking at the event.

ALTERNATIVES

Participants report on:
1 A royal visit at which no expense has been spared;
2 A football or sports event, during which violence breaks out;
3 A Prime Minister's visit, during which she is bombarded with rotten fruit;
4 A fox-hunting event, which is attended by people trying to stop it;
5 A foreigner being deported;
6 Queuing for the January sales in a snowstorm;
7 Teachers or nurses going on strike.

COMMENT

Look through a daily newspaper, pick out any current happening and have participants imagine a similar event and write their own reports on the subject. Alternatively, have them report on an event from their own experience.

SEARCH

PROCEDURE

Each person thinks back to an occasion when they wanted something but had to conduct a search for it. It may have been a summer shirt, a tie of a particular colour, an antique item, a perfect gift for someone, or something which had been lost. They write down why the item was wanted and the details of the search, including obstacles and how they were overcome. They conclude by telling where and how the item was found and describe the feeling on finding it.

DISCUSSION

Can group members think of any other ways in which the search could have been made? Looking back, do the searchers think there was anything they could have done differently? Is life a continual search for ideas, love, security and the rest?

ALTERNATIVES

Participants write about a personal search for:

1 friendship;
2 love;
3 knowledge;

4 a job;
5 security;
6 happiness.

COMMENT

Have participants describe what they are predominantly searching for in their lives at present. How do they aim to find it?

PORTRAITS 1

PROCEDURE

Participants write a physical history of themselves. They start by describing their physique as a child and how they felt about it. Were they shy, envious, curious? Did they see themselves as weak, strong and so on? How did their physique develop as they grew and how did this influence their thoughts, confidence and well-being? In life, what has affected their health for good and bad? Include habits. The historical portrait should end with a physical description of the way they see themselves now and how this affects their life.

DISCUSSION

Does physique reflect and influence the way we feel inside? Does this mean we should look after our physical well-being? Compare ideas and discuss ways and means of keeping fit.

ALTERNATIVES

Participants write a historical portrait, describing:

1 How they have developed and grown into the personality they are now.

2 How their education, knowledge, skills and interests have developed up to the present.

3 How they have fitted into their way of life and got on with people. With whom and what have they felt comfortable? When have they felt at odds with the world?

4 Happenings which have influenced their lives and over which they have (a) had control; (b) not had control.

5 Their lives, written from the viewpoint of someone else — a school teacher, friend or doctor — who has seen them develop up to the present.

COMMENT

Use this exercise in conjunction with *Portraits 2*.

PORTRAITS 2

PROCEDURE

Participants look in a mirror and write a description of themselves: their clothes, neatness, build, posture, skin texture and what other people would assume from looking at them. They then write, describing what they would want other people to think about them from what they see and how they would like to look in the future.

DISCUSSION

Compare what has been written by each person with the way other members of the group see them. Do they agree that the way participants plan to present themselves in the future will have the desired effect? Is it realistic? Explore ideas and ways and means of working towards a new image.

ALTERNATIVES

Participants write about:

1 What it is like to be them at the moment. How they feel inside and how they think other people see them. When this is completed they describe how they would like to feel and be seen in the future.

2 The worst possible future which could develop from their present situation, followed by the ideal future.

3 How they would like to develop as a person in the future. Would they perhaps become more open-minded, patient or relaxed?

4 How they would like their education, knowledge, skills and interests to develop. They describe how this could be achieved and conclude with a portrait of themselves as a success.

5 How they see themselves fitting into their future surroundings and what they will be.

6 What future events they anticipate which will influence their lives and over which they will (a) have control; (b) not have control. How will they cope with the second contingency?

7 Their lives, written from the viewpoint of someone else — a school teacher, friend or doctor — as this person will view them at a specific time in the future.

COMMENT

Use this exercise in conjunction with *Portraits 1*.

MEMORABILIA

PROCEDURE

Group members think about objects they would like to leave behind when they die, in order that their great grandchildren will learn something about them. Each person then writes, describing the objects, how they feel they would be interpreted and how each object would represent them to the inheritor.

DISCUSSION

How does each person wish to be remembered? Compare viewpoints. If members could leave just one piece of advice, what would it be? Does any of the above tell participants anything about themselves and what they want from life?

ALTERNATIVES

Members write about:
1   What they would like to have known about — and inherited from — their great grandparents or ancestors.
2   Objects they would leave for future mankind to give an impression of life today.
3   Objects they would send into space to inhabitants of another planet to represent mankind.

COMMENT

Ask members to include an item which shows a sense of humour.

CONFLICTING INTERESTS

PROCEDURE

Each person writes about the conflict between self-interest and the interests of other people. What is it that pulls them towards doing something for someone else? What makes them resist? They may want to say they love someone, but something stops them. What? They may want to do someone a kindness, but resist. Each participant thinks about one such incident in their own lives which has involved giving of themselves or time, or making a sacrifice. They express how it felt, explain both parts of the conflict as they experienced it and describe the final outcome.

DISCUSSION

Are there occasions when the interests of other people should come first? When is this? On what occasions should people put themselves first? Is to do this selfish? Does any of the above tell anyone anything about themselves and their ability to get along with other people and make friends? Compare viewpoints.

ALTERNATIVES

1 Participants write about the conflict of interest within themselves when money, property, valuables or something of a material nature is involved. They recall or invent an incident.

2 How is this balance of interests affected when participants are confronted with a strange situation they have not anticipated? Each person describes one such occasion, the immediate inner reaction and the later outcome.

3 Members describe the balance of inner conflict when they are confronted with something they do not want to do or dislike doing.

COMMENT

Using any of the above alternatives, have participants write a dialogue between two characters, one representing self-interest and the other the opposing interests of someone else, as it might be argued in an inner conflict.

OPPOSING EMOTIONS

PROCEDURE

Have group members envisage themselves in a situation where they show tenderness or think back to an actual event. It can be a personal display of tenderness to a family member, a friend, a stranger or an injured animal. Participants describe what evokes the tenderness and the experience itself. After ten to fifteen minutes ask participants to write about themselves in a situation where they are expressing anger.

DISCUSSION

Which display of emotion reveals the real person? Is it possible to experience feelings of tenderness and anger at the same time? Can members recall any such situations experienced? If two or more emotions are experienced at one time, what contradictions, tensions and pressures emerge? Describe these.

ALTERNATIVES

Participants write about situations involving other opposing emotions.
1   Love and jealousy;
2   Happiness and sadness;
3   Being silly and being serious;
4   Approval and disapproval;
5   Courage and fear;
6   Self-sacrifice and selfishness;
7   Sympathy and dislike.

COMMENT

Many other opposites can be used. As another alternative call out a different emotion every few minutes. Participants react by writing their experiences of the emotions. Members can, of course, choose two or three emotions to write about from a given list.

LIFE JOURNEY

PROCEDURE

Request that group members imagine their lives as a journey on which, at various points, they have to change means and/or direction of conveyance. Life may have started on a bicycle, changed to a car which, in turn, might have been traded in for a newer model, then the car could be left at an airport for the luxury of an aeroplane, and so on. Participants write describing each part of the journey, change of direction and/or transport and what they were thinking and feeling at these times.

DISCUSSION

Does the type of transport reflect appropriately the way the person was thinking and feeling? Let members comment. Does the choice of transport for each part of life reflect the way participants saw themselves, how they imagine others might have seen them or how they wanted to appear?

ALTERNATIVES

Participants write:

1   Placing emphasis on where they are going and the setting of fresh goals at each change.
2   Concentrating on the reasons and causes for each change of transport.
3   Concerning one change of transport in their lives. They describe causes, adapting to change, setting of fresh goals and the new destination. Also, have them include the way others see their new mode of transport. Are they envious, pleased, dismayed or what?

COMMENT

It is useful to discuss different modes of transport or to provide a list before starting to write. Examples: train, jumbo jet, glider, pram, ship, rowing-boat, horse and cart, family car, sports car and so on.

COLOUR

PROCEDURE

Participants write about the way colour has affected their lives, what colour means to them and how they use it. Which colour is dominant? What feelings and emotions are aroused by different colours? How does this influence the way the colour is seen? With what colours do the participants surround themselves? What colour do they see as representing themselves? What colours are associated with different events in the participants' lives?

DISCUSSION

Do people discard colours associated with bad times or things of which they do not want to be reminded? How does colour affect all our lives? How can it be used as a positive force to create an environment which is comfortable and good? Have other members comment on the colours participants see as representing themselves. Does everyone have the same emotional reaction to all colours? Compare.

ALTERNATIVES

Participants write about:
1   Smells in their lives;
2   Sounds in their lives.

COMMENT

Try calling out a different colour every few minutes and have participants write a reaction or association with it. Read out and compare. Also, use this exercise as an inspiration for poetry.

ADVERTS

PROCEDURE

Make up, or cut from a newspaper personal column, an appropriate advert asking for a companion or friend. Instruct participants to answer the advert, extolling their virtues and abilities. Request that they think about the needs, interests and so on of the person who has placed the advert.

DISCUSSION

Have each person read out. Encourage other group members to add aspects and abilities they see in the reader and which have been missed out in the answer.

ALTERNATIVES

1   Have group members place their own adverts, writing a few paragraphs requesting a friend or companion.
2   Vary the type of advert. Advertise for someone to share a holiday or someone with whom to share a house; as a prospective tenant appealing for someone who might make an ideal landlord or a prospective parent looking for an ideal son or daughter; as someone looking for an ideal employer and so on.
3   Have fun by making the advert an appeal for someone to climb the Alps, cross the Sahara on a camel, become a revolutionary, go on a joy-ride to the moon or something similar. The more funny or ridiculous the better.
4   Have members describe a shop-window which has their personal qualities on display. What needs to be added to make the display better?

COMMENT

An exercise which is fun and makes the participants feel good.

DIFFERENCES & SIMILARITIES

PROCEDURE

Most people like to think of themselves as being different from others in some respects. Ask participants to ponder about other group members and write comparing one of them to themselves. Have them consider appearance, dress, way of life, ambition, outlook on life, physique, accent, background, education, way of thinking, interests, marital status, and so on.

DISCUSSION

When individuals read out their pieces have the other members comment on whether or not they agree with the differences cited. If not, how do they see the differences? Discuss individuality and the things which make everyone unique.

ALTERNATIVES

Participants write:

1 Concerning differences between themselves and other members of their family, friends or colleagues at work.
2 Regarding similarities or things they have in common with another member of the group, their family, a friend or a workmate.
3 Reflecting on the qualities they would like to have in common with other group members, their family, friends or workmates.
4 About the things they have in common with other participants, friends or workmates which they would prefer not to have. Have them explain why and how this would alter their lives.

COMMENT

This exercise helps members to consider and value their own individuality. Also, it aids members to exchange views of each other.

WITH THESE HANDS

PROCEDURE

Group members inspect their own hands and write:

a) giving an overall impression and then a detailed description of skin, texture, lines and so on;

b) saying how their hands feel when they are idle and at various times of the day;

c) describing how they use their hands for work, hobbies, communicating, gardening, washing-up, shaking hands and any other things they do with them;

d) what they think and feel about their hands;

e) what other people can discern about them from their hands. How do they imagine other people see them?

DISCUSSION

Encourage group members to look at, touch and comment on other people's hands. How does sensitivity of hands vary when doing different things? For example, using them for gardening as compared with touching someone affectionately? How would a person's ability and life be affected if they were without one or both hands? Is there anything group members would like to be able to do with their hands which they feel they cannot? Why?

ALTERNATIVES

1 They write about their arms, legs, feet, head or face in the same manner.

2 This time have them write about the complete body.

3 Set each group member a simple task or exercise to do, concentrating on the use of hands, feet or the whole body. Immediately afterwards, have them write a description of their hands or whatever is engaged in the task.

COMMENT

A self-awareness exercise which is good fun.

A PRIVATE PERSON

PROCEDURE

Participants write about the private side of themselves — the side no one sees. Is it a secret self which resists probing? Does it hide fears, thoughts, loves, hates which cannot be shared? How different is that person to the one presented to the world? Does the private self feel different from the public person? Encourage participants to write about at least one thought, fear, love or belief which they have never shared before.

DISCUSSION

How did everyone feel about revealing something private? Why do fears, emotions, thoughts and feelings become buried and impossible to discuss? Share experiences. Can sharing the private person help others understand? Is it appropriate to share everything about yourself with everyone?

ALTERNATIVES

Participants write about:

1   The part of themselves shared with a few — or just one — close friend.
2   The part of themselves shared with acquaintances.
3   The part of themselves shared with work colleagues.
4   Being alone. What it means to them. How they cope and how they feel about it.
5   Being with other people. What part does this play in their lives? Is it important? Do they need other people? If so, is this from choice or dependence?

COMMENT

Combine the described exercise with alternatives (1) (2) and (3), allowing participants a few minutes only to write on each. Do the same with alternatives (4) and (5).

WOUNDS

PROCEDURE

For this exercise, participants think back to an occasion when a friend did something to hurt or wound them. The act may not have been a deliberate one. It could have been inflicted in anger, thoughtlessness or in ignorance. Each person writes about the experience.

DISCUSSION

Did everyone let the person inflicting the wound know about the hurt by comment or action? If not, why not? What do the writers imagine the offending person's reaction could be towards the idea of hurting them? Should we suffer in silence? Compare and discuss ways of coping with hurts and wounds. How does the act alter the way the victim perceives the friend?

ALTERNATIVES

Participants write about:

1 A wound they inflicted on a friend;
2 A wound given to them by a member of their family;
3 A wound they inflicted on a family member.

COMMENT

The wounds need not be horrific, but merely a snub or a betrayal of a minor trust.

EULOGY

PROCEDURE

Group members look back on their past and pick out some highlights from their lives: what they have achieved, what they have contributed to the lives of husbands, wives, sons, daughters, friends and society. They then write a eulogy, to be published after their death, describing them as they would like to be remembered. Encourage the use of positive attributes, such as having a sense of humour, being hard-working, loyal, courageous, tidy and so on.

DISCUSSION

Does the way participants would like to be remembered differ from the way they believe they appear to others now? In what way? Can the gap between the two be bridged? Have members comment.

ALTERNATIVES

Participants write:

1 Expressing how they think they will be remembered;
2 A eulogy for a husband, wife, son, daughter, mother, father, friend, or someone admired who is still alive;
3 A eulogy for another member of the group, emphasising positive attributes.

COMMENT

This is another exercise which lends itself to poetry.

IMAGES

PROCEDURE

Group members consider the image they create by the way they dress and then write, giving thought to:

a) whether it is a deliberate image they consciously pursue;

b) how successful they imagine they are at projecting that image;

c) how they want to be seen;

d) what they imagine other people think of them from the way they dress.

DISCUSSION

How important is creating an accurate image? Is it more important on some occasions, such as going for an interview, than at other times? How do other group members see each individual? Do their impressions go along with the written description?

ALTERNATIVES

Participants write, describing:

1 Another member of the group, concentrating on the image created by the way they dress.

2 A friend or another family member in the same fashion.

3 Their own room, house, garden or car, giving attention to the personal image projected by it.

4 Their own image — this time, created by their mannerisms, the way they speak and the way in which they express views and opinions.

COMMENT

Many other exercises promoting an awareness of self-image can be added, examining, for example, how participants organise their day, how they spend their spare time, their attitudes, their job, and so on.

THROUGH OTHER EYES

PROCEDURE

Group members envisage and write about themselves and their way of life as seen through the eyes of someone new to them. This could be anyone who might appear on their doorstep: a salesman, insurance man or plumber, for example. Things to bear in mind while writing are:

a) appearance;

b) sense of humour, or lack of it;

c) life-style;

d) ability to cope with life;

e) ability to give and receive friendship;

f) ability to get along with others;

g) job and interests.

DISCUSSION

Compare the written comments with other group members' views of that person.

ALTERNATIVES

Participants write about themselves, imagining being seen through the eyes of:

1 A child: this could be a son, daughter or a visiting child;

2 Someone older: perhaps a grandparent, parent or an older guest;

3 Someone who likes or loves the participant;

4 Someone who dislikes the participant.

COMMENT

These exercises enable participants to see themselves anew, expand self-knowledge and give a new angle of vision.

INTERRUPTIONS

PROCEDURE

Group members imagine they have got very dirty from working hard. They anticipate a nice hot bath or shower. But each time they go to the bathroom and begin to undress they are interrupted and have to deal with a problem. First a wife or husband wants them to do something, then, perhaps, they have to attend to a child, after which the dog escapes from the garden, and so on. Participants write, describing each interruption, how they feel and react every time it happens. When this has been done, have members finish off by stating how their reaction has made them look in the eyes of their family.

DISCUSSION

Compare various members' reactions. Who becomes angry, irritable, tense or frustrated? How does this affect other people when it happens? How do members cope and control any outbursts? Does anyone see the comic side of the situations, during or after the event?

ALTERNATIVES

Participants write about:

1 A similar experience they have had;
2 Going to answer the phone or to make an important call and being interrupted;
3 Going to open the front door to an important visitor when the interruptions occur;
4 Preparing for an important engagement with continual interruptions.

COMMENT

As well as showing how individuals act in these circumstances, these exercises can be excellent for stimulating imagination and humour.

RUNNING AWAY

PROCEDURE

Ask participants to think of something in life which would make them feel like running away. Perhaps a problem they do not want to face, a person, a situation or a minor cause of irritation or frustration. Participants write, describing what they would run from, how they would react and where they would go.

DISCUSSION

How does each person deal with and overcome such feelings when they occur? Is tension and anger created? Does talking about how they feel act as a relief? Are there occasions when it is necessary to run away? How do these feelings affect the way participants see themselves? Do they fear exposing them?

ALTERNATIVES

1   Participants write about a threatening situation from which they ran, or wanted to run.
2   Invent a threatening situation: a burglary, being followed, being threatened, being at a public event when violence breaks out, being intimidated by a neighbour or fellow worker and so on. Participants write, imagining themselves in the given situation and describing how they would react initially and the final outcome.
3   Participants describe a fear they have, such as fear of spiders, dogs, mice, the dark, answering the door at night, open spaces or crowded rooms. How does the fear affect them? How do they cope with it? Have them write about one incident.

COMMENT

To lighten the mood and add a sense of fun, ask writers to exaggerate out of all proportion the thing they do not want to face and their reactions to it.

VOICES

PROCEDURE

Individual members write about their own voices. They describe how they sound, whether they speak with an accent, and the changes in their voices according to mood and what they are doing. Have they difficulty pronouncing some words? How do their voices react to different people and situations? Have them include the way it feels when they are speaking and what impression they think they make on other people. How do they try to use their voices and do they feel they succeed? Has the sound of their voices changed over the years? In what way? How do they feel about their own voices?

DISCUSSION

In each case, add to what has been written by encouraging members to comment on each others' voices, giving opinions on how each voice sounds to them. How much can you learn about someone by listening to their voice?

ALTERNATIVES

Participants write about:
1   Another member's voice;
2   Type of voices disliked;
3   Types of voices liked;
4   Voices of friends or other members of their family;
5   A voice they would like to have.

COMMENT

Before starting the exercise, have members practise using different voice tones: calm, condescending, angry, happy, melodious and so on. Also, it is useful to make a tape recording so that participants can hear the sound of their own voices.

Producing a Magazine or Newspaper

What follows is intended only as a guide; the process need not be carried out in the order indicated here, nor do all the decisions have to be made before beginning. However, in order to succeed, the group leader should be aware of what is involved and be able to adapt as necessary to suit the needs of the group.

BENEFITS

The thrill of seeing the increase in motivation and enthusiasm among group members, when they realise that there is an end-product and audience in mind, is worth the effort involved. Other benefits are:

▶ an increase in confidence
▶ a better self-image
▶ a sense of involvement
▶ learning to communicate
▶ sharing knowledge and experience
▶ learning accuracy
▶ a sense of achievement
▶ learning to make friends
▶ learning to solve problems
▶ learning to make decisions
▶ an ability to sustain effort
▶ learning organisation
▶ learning presentation
▶ experience of working in a team.

The above is not an exhaustive list. Perhaps the biggest benefit to group members is the overall experience itself and seeing their writing in print. This indicates to them that they are being taken seriously and that what they have to say is important.

THE GROUP LEADERS' COMMITMENT

Taking on the production of a booklet or magazine is a big commitment for the group leader. There are likely to be many problems and some difficult decisions to make. Once committed, there can be no backing down without crushing the enthusiasm, motivation and new-found impetus generated in those involved. Before the decision is made to go ahead, thought should be given to the following:

a)   Time. Producing a magazine, especially one which has to be put together on, say, a quarterly basis, can consume a large amount of time. Will other commitments allow enough time over a long period?

b) Sustained effort. To produce even a pamphlet, real effort and willing, consistent support will be necessary.

c) Experience. If this is the first such project undertaken it is better to gain experience by doing wall posters first, progressing to pamphlets, a small booklet and, lastly, a magazine produced on a regular basis. It is recommended that the group's confidence be built up in this progression. However, if group leaders are experienced and know the problems to be faced they may decide differently.

CHOICE OF APPROACH

The choice of approach will be influenced by the group leaders' commitment, the aims and purpose of the group, the members' abilities and the facilities available. It will probably be reduced to one of four choices:

1 The leaders take a prominent role: planning, making most of the decisions, allocating jobs, seeing that members fulfil commitments, advising, teaching and so on.

2 The leaders give advice only. The group members plan, make the decisions, allocate jobs and, in effect, organise the project themselves. They call on the leaders only for advice, use them as arbitrators in disputes and for other matters outside the control of the group.

3 The leaders work as one of the group, on an equal-role basis.

4 The leaders work on a mixed-role basis. They first take a prominent role, then gradually allow the members, as they gain confidence, to begin making the decisions. They continue on an equal-role basis, or as advisers, stepping back into a prominent role as necessity dictates, in order to sustain momentum, continuity and the success of the group.

Most groups — especially those new to this type of project — will prefer the leader to work with them on a mixed-role basis. Personally, I have always found that working on an equal-role basis — as often as possible — is the most satisfying, both for myself and the group members. However, circumstances and the abilities of the participants may dictate otherwise.

COUNTING THE COST

Producing a magazine or booklet can be costly. How much cash is needed will depend on the magnitude of the project. Where will the money come from? If the group is independent, the whole sum may have to be found. Working within an organisation, such as a hospital, can be helpful, as photocopying facilities are usually available.

Money can be raised by raffles, car-boot sales, bingo sessions and the like. And, of course, a charge can be made for the booklet or magazine. Opinions may differ or be affected by the environment in which the project is undertaken, but my feelings are that a charge should be made, no matter how small. There is an extra boost to the ego and a feeling of satisfaction if someone is willing to pay to read your work. It gives an added feeling of importance and writers know they are being taken seriously. This is a decision which the group can make for themselves.

FOR WHOM ARE YOU WRITING?

It is important to know your audience. This will help later, when it is necessary to decide what to include in the publication and how it is to be presented. For example, a newspaper published in a hospital environment for patients might include details of hospital facilities available for use by patients and articles on hospital life, personalities and so on. Whereas a magazine for sale outside the hospital would concentrate more on topics of interest to a different readership. These topics might include subjects such as gardening, local activities, local personalities or gossip.

VISITING A PUBLISHER

Contact a local newspaper or publishing firm if possible. Tell them what you are doing and ask that the group be allowed to visit. Most local publishers will be only too pleased to arrange this and to show how the whole process — from receiving a story, through editing, to final copy — is done by professionals. A visit will have many benefits, the chief ones being:

a) It demonstrates clearly what is required and cuts out lecturing to group members;

b) Members feel better about changing their own writing after seeing professionals' work being edited;

c)   Interest is stimulated by the excitement of meeting and talking with people who are enthusiastic about writing.

Afterwards, discuss the visit. Go through the whole process: writing, selecting material, editing, deciding layout, the actual production, distribution and selling. Examining each part of the production will help group members to deal — and come to terms — with various problems which arise. If it is not possible to arrange a visit, invite someone along to the group who can explain the process, or get the group to research and then discuss it.

DECISIONS TO MAKE

It will be necessary for members to talk about and decide:

a)   The importance of editing; what it entails and whether or not their magazine warrants it. What is to be done about grammar and spelling? Is it appropriate not to correct this in some instances?

b)   To reject or not to reject contributions. What are the implications of rejection to individuals? How is this to be handled? Will help be given to bring the material up to standard?

c)   How the material is to be selected. Is each piece to be read out at group meetings and comments made, or will each be taken home in turn by members?

d)   Whether deadlines are necessary. If the intention is to produce a magazine every month or quarter, work will need to be submitted early enough to enable the magazine to come out on time. While this is not essential for a booklet or pamphlet, it is better to set a deadline because it acts as a spur. The very fact that other group members expect the work to be done provides incentive.

e)   A title for the magazine. The title should indicate the content, set the tone and also attract the intended reader. A tall order indeed!

f)   Content. Are contributions to be selected from writings which have resulted from exercises in this book? Will these need working upon, shaping and rewriting to suit the publication? Perhaps most pieces will need to be specially written. Can anyone in the group provide illustrations? What is the content to be — articles, stories, anecdotes, puzzles? Who is going to contribute what? Have the members browse through a wide variety of magazines to see what material is used and note the different ways each subject is angled to suit the intended reader.

Here is a list of ideas

- nature articles
- crosswords
- hobbies
- viewpoints
- personal experiences
- a day in your life
- poetry and verse
- cookery
- baking
- quizzes
- local customs
- jokes
- quotations
- tips for the housewife
- beauty
- the family
- sport
- a woman's world
- diets
- the countryside
- focus on clubs, societies and so on
- first aid
- bargains
- presents
- keep fit
- book reviews
- common fallacies
- good news
- relationships
- current issues
- what's new
- women/men of history
- therapy
- senior citizens' corner
- TV and film review
- local history
- fashion
- a funny thing happened
- success story
- personalities
- soap box
- problem page
- gardening
- DIY
- travel
- famous people profile
- letters
- finance
- using local facilities
- the home
- yearly festivals
- health
- a man's world
- competitions
- pets' corner
- motoring
- legal affairs
- shopping hints
- public services
- anniversaries
- interviews
- how to . . .
- mysteries
- riddles
- careers
- ideas for holidays
- children's corner
- coming events
- nostalgia
- opinions

SOME MORE QUESTIONS TO ANSWER

1 How many pages will the magazine contain?
2 What size will each page be?
3 Is the intention to print on one or both sides of the paper?
4 Are photocopying or printing facilities available?
5 Will the pages be folded and stapled in the centre or will they be flat and stapled in one corner?
6 What sort of front cover will the magazine have?
7 Who will do the typing?

ADVICE, SUPPORT AND ENCOURAGEMENT

One of the rewards of producing a magazine or newspaper is the help, support and encouragement group members can give each other. The enthusiasm becomes infectious, the momentum exhilarating. Of course, there will be individual dark moments, but a group encouraged in a positive way, with the group leader highlighting what is good and showing how improvements can be made — rather than offering criticism or repeatedly pointing out errors — will overcome these moments.

Eventually the selection, editing, typing, printing, stapling and distribution will be completed. Along the way friends will have been made, problems shared and the thrill of communicating with the reader experienced. It then only remains for the group to have a discussion or writing session to assess what has been learned and gained, what felt about the total experience.

Good luck — have lots of fun!

Alphabetical List of exercises